The Psychology of Society

The Psychology
of Society

by

MORRIS GINSBERG

D.Lit., F.B.A.

Professor Emeritus of Sociology
in the University of London

BARNES & NOBLE INC
NEW YORK

PRINTED IN GREAT BRITAIN

Contents

	Introduction to the ninth edition	vii
	Introduction to the eighth edition	xxv
I	The General Nature of Instinct	1
II	Instinct in Society	13
III	The Role of Reason and Will	29
IV	The Theory of a Social or Group Mind	39
V	The Conception of a General Will	60
VI	Racial and National Characteristics	82
VII	Tradition	90
VIII	Community, Associations and Institutions	101
IX	The Psychology of the Crowd	111
X	The Public and Public Opinion	119
XI	The Psychology of Organization and Democracy	132
	Conclusion	144
	Bibliography	147
	Appendix I *Psycho-Analysis and Sociology*	151
	Appendix II *On Prejudice*	167
	Index	185

Introduction to the Ninth Edition

THIS BOOK WAS first published in 1921 and has been reprinted several times without revision. In considering a new edition at the request of Messrs Methuen I have decided not to attempt a recast but to let the text speak for itself from the past. It seemed desirable, however, to add in appendices two papers published in the intervening period bearing on the topics dealt with in the book and to write a new introductory chapter indicating my present attitude to its central themes.

In essentials the book was concerned with two groups of problems: How is the individual related to society? And, How are the irrational or non-rational elements of the mind related to the rational? In the climate of thought prevailing at the time the two themes were closely interwoven. The questions that both raised were expressed in the form, what are the elements in the human mind which determine social relations, and, conversely, how do these social relations react on the mind? To answer these questions it was necessary to arrive at some notion of the role of intelligence and instinct, will and impulse, and of the way in which these are affected as they affect the action of mind upon mind in society.

Comparative psychology and especially the study of animal behaviour was then beginning to throw new light on the interpretation of human conduct. Psychological hedonism, the theory that all action is ultimately to be traced to anticipation of pleasure and pain, had been philosophically refuted by Bishop Butler, who showed conclusively that the springs of action were to be found in 'particular propensities' which 'tend towards their objects' rather than to the feelings attending their satisfaction.[1] The new psychology effectively reinforced this refutation. It was

[1] *Butler's Works*, ed. Gladstone, vol. II. XI. 3.

shown that pleasure and pain had the function of confirming and controlling rather than of initiating impulses, and that, even in those cases in which feeling does not appear to depend upon prior appetition or want, we might assume the existence of susceptibilities or interests stimulating attention or action without which the feelings would not supervene.

The theory that gained most support for a time was that based on the concept of instinct. This was due in part to the growing influence of evolutionary ideas and the desire to link human with animal behaviour. Reinforcement came later from another source, that of psycho-analysis which required a theory of inborn drives in dealing with conflict, repression and sublimation. In any event, the instinct theory, especially in the form given to it by McDougall, came to be widely used in the various fields of social inquiry, e.g. education, industry, social and political organization. There is no doubt that it was wildly abused. The term instinct was allowed to run riot and was used to cover all sorts of actions, however contingent and variable, provided they could be assumed to have some sort of hereditary basis and could be contrasted with the rational or consciously purposive.

The theory, however, very soon came under attack. From the side of philosophy it was dismissed as pseudo-scientific, substituting occult qualities or mere naming for explanation and analysis. The behaviourists and their sympathizers objected to it, at any rate, as applied to man, as incapable of experimental verification. Seen in retrospect, the scepticism with which the whole notion of instinct in man was viewed by psychologists had two roots. In the first place, it formed part of what may be called the flight from the mind characteristic of the early behaviourists. To them the use of such notions as impulse, effort, end or purpose was anathema. Connected with this was the wish to believe that human conduct could be changed at will by changes in the environment. It was clear to me at the time that the belief in the omnipotence of the environment, like the eighteenth-century belief in the indefinite perfectibility of man, was mistaken and that it would inevitably provoke a reversal to the opposite view of the overriding importance of inborn factors. In fact, the arguments swayed to and fro, entangled in the wider but equally confused controversy of nature *versus* nurture. As far as animal behaviour is concerned the concept of instinct has in recent work been resuscitated by the ethologists. There seems to be general agreement among them that instincts are (1) innate, that is inherited and specific; (2) that they usually involve complex action patterns; (3) that they are evoked by complex environmental situations to which the senses are inherently attuned, so that the animal tends to attend to particular objects or to seek for them with great perseverance and sometimes intelligence. (Cf. W. H. Thorpe, *Learning and Instinct in Animals*, 1956, p. 17.)

In its application to man the rejection of the concept of instinct was never as thoroughgoing as its critics pretended. They usually allowed it to come back by a side-door under another name, e.g. innate tendencies, wishes or 'drives'. They were right in maintaining that instinct in the sense of inborn fixed action patterns was not very useful in explaining human behaviour. They were further right in their criticism of the various lists of human instincts which had been suggested. These were open to the objection that they included tendencies so diverse as the very general instinct of self-preservation, and instincts like those of sex and maternity, in which it was more plausible to maintain that there was an innate drive organizing behaviour on lines which were in general, though not in detail, innately determined, and others again, such as acquisitiveness, based largely on doubtful analogies drawn from animal behaviour and mostly from species not very near to man. Despite all this, it seems to me that the conception of instinct in its application to human behaviour is still useful, first, as a 'limiting' notion applicable to modes of behaviour according as they approach the type of action in which both the end or object and the mode of its attainment are mainly determined by heredity. On this view ends innately determined come in the course of experience to be apprehended with varying degrees of clarity, to be related to each other, and to be controlled and checked in the interests of relatively wide and comprehensive purposes. ⌐Secondly, the notion of instinct is required to describe forms of behaviour in which drives are in conflict with each other and can challenge, though not necessarily defeat, rational control⌐ This seems to be the use of the notion of instinct found especially helpful in psychopathology, and it is one which has been largely ignored by the critics. It may be noted further that it survives even among the Neo-Freudians, e.g. Karen Horney and Erich Fromm, despite their criticism of what they take to be Freud's failure to make sufficient allowances for variations in cultural conditions.[1]

In dealing with the relation of instinct and intelligence I adopted what may be best described as a theory of ascending levels of development, and I tried to show that at all stages conation, cognition and feeling are closely interwoven. Thus instinct, desire and volition have each their corresponding cognitive and affective structure. On the instinctive level there is perception of objects directly present to the senses and there is a feeling tone sustaining the chain of acts. On the level of desire the cognitive structure is at least that of 'free ideas', involving the power of recall and of anticipating future situations. It is characteristic of desire that there is a gap between the impulse and its fulfilment. Hence in connexion with desire we find emotions which Shand has called the emotions of desire – hope, anxiety, confidence, disappointment, despair – which cannot arise until the subject is able to look backward and forward. Finally, in the stage of volition the cognitive structure is that of analytic comparison, general concepts and principles and on the affective side the organization of emotional dispositions into sentiments. Volition implies the action of the self as a permanent entity, having continuity and identity, endowed with the capacity of forming or accepting general rules of action and of considering and weighing alternatives both as regards fact and value. The act of volition is on this view a new act and not merely the triumph of the stronger impulse or desire. This act,

[1] For a full discussion of recent work on instinct *see* Ronald Fletcher, *Instinct in Man*, 1957.

however, is not due to a unique factor but is a response of the more organized systems of desire and the emotional and cognitive dispositions connected with them[On this view then the function of intelligence is (1) to bring the ends of the impulses into consciousness; (2) to relate them to one another so as to form comprehensive purposes; (3) to control and regulate partial and immediate impulses and desires with the aid of sentiments or systems of sentiments and (4) to vary the means as growing experience shows what is most effective.]

The theory of levels of conation seemed to me important as against the view which was gaining ground that the ends of action were given by the hereditary structure and that the function of reason was confined to the discovery of the means needed to attain them, aided in the choice of the means, as McDougall insisted, by pleasure and pain. It was equally important, on the other hand, to avoid the opposite extreme of claiming for reason powers of its own, capable of initiating action by itself and of controlling impulse and desire, as it were, from above. The effect of my argument was that we had not to choose between Hume's view, supposed to be strengthened by the psychology of instinct and the unconscious, of reason as the slave of the passions and Kant's view as independent of them and overriding them. The lesson of comparative psychology was, it seemed to me, that cognition, feeling and conation are in varying degrees intertwined at all stages of behaviour. The primary needs of the organism are laid down in the hereditary structure, but they are transformed by the growth of knowledge and the influence of social factors. As the individual matures he discovers that what he wants and what he needs are not necessarily the same. Analytic reflection is required to reveal what it is in the objects we pursue that we desire, and how it is that we seek satisfaction where it is not to be found. New needs, purposes and ideals are generated with the growth of knowledge of human capacities and the opportunities that nature provides for their fulfilment. The individual's tastes and wants are shaped and conditioned by social factors. Far from being simply 'given' the ends of action are complex and variable. They cannot be attributed to feeling or cognition 'in themselves'. There are desires which are only possible at certain levels of cognitive development and there are thoughts which are only possible at certain levels of emotional intensity.

In reflecting on these arguments after an interval of forty years it is clear that even in the form in which I have just restated them they are much too general to be effective as against the anti-intellectualists or anti-rationalists. In any event the distrust of the part of reason in human affairs has persisted and even gained in strength. This has taken many forms and I propose now to discuss some of them briefly. There is first the impact of psycho-analysis. This has often been taken as implying that the ultimate sources of action are to be found in unconscious drives and that what reason does is to 'rationalize', that is, to present the impulses in a form acceptable to the conscious mind. As an account of Freud's own views of the role of reason this is absurd. To begin with Freud had great faith in the power of rational inquiry. He dismisses subjectivist or relativist views of knowledge as 'intellectual nihilism'. (*New Introductory Lectures*, p. 224.) Though our knowledge of nature is affected by the structure of the mind, this does not make knowledge necessarily subjective, since the structure of the mind can itself be scientifically investigated and the errors due to subjective factors allowed for. In Freud's own account of mental structure the role of reason is by no means insignificant. The 'ego' is that part of the mind which is influenced by perception and reasoning and helps the organism to act in accordance with the 'reality principle' or in other words, to learn from experience. It is true that the 'id', that is, the untamed impulses, is said to have no organization and to persist unchanged. But this cannot be intended to be taken strictly, for we are also told that the ego is the organized portion of the id (*Inhibition, Symptoms and Anxiety*, p. 32), so that some part of the id at any rate is organized. Furthermore, the ego is said to make for unity and synthesis. To it, therefore, are assigned functions which in general psychology are assigned to 'reason'. On the therapeutic side, it is clear that it is taken for granted that the non-rational elements of the mind are subject to rational control. The aims of analysis are said to be: 'To strengthen the ego, to make it more independent of the super-ego, to widen its field of vision and so to extend its organization that it can take over new portions of the id. Where id was, there shall ego be'. (*New Introductory Lectures*, p. 106.) Elsewhere hopes are held out for a rational ethic. The ultimate ideal is said to be 'the primacy of reason' and on the moral side 'the brotherhood of man and the reduction of suffering'.

How is it then that Freud's theory has been described as anti-rationalist? Apart from errors due to misunderstanding, there seems to have been a failure to distinguish between the ideal functions of reason and its actual operation in the lives of men. As regards the former Freud differs in no way from other rationalists; as regards the latter his outlook is pessimistic. He and his followers lay great stress on the imperviousness of the instincts to the influence of the ego and the difficulty the ego has in maintaining its superiority over them. His conception of the history of civilization is even more sombre. Eros is pitted against Thanatos and the antagonism will in all probability never be overcome. Even the love instincts are divided among themselves. The striving for happiness comes into conflict with the impulse towards union with others. Repression or renunciation is essential to culture, yet cannot achieve liberation or harmony. His views on the future of mankind are, however, purely speculative. To substantiate them it would be necessary to undertake a wide comparative study of the role of repression in the history of culture, in particular, of what Freud calls the 'cultural super-ego' as represented in the ethics of the higher religions. Such a study, as Freud well knew, was only in its initial stages.

Pareto, to whom anti-rationalists also appeal, is far less cautious than Freud. He thinks himself justified in concluding that while in the arts and sciences and in economic production reason has on the whole gained in strength, it has not affected political and social activities to any great extent. But this is not substantiated by anything like a methodical survey of the history of law, morals or social and political institutions. He makes a great parade of what he calls the 'logico-experimental method', but particularly when he comes to deal with the dynamics of social change, the empirical evidence given is very slight, the facts cited being hardly more than illustrative of the hypotheses put forward. In any event, if we agree that there is no law of human progress, and no one nowadays believes in automatic progress or in unlimited perfectibility, we must insist as against Pareto, that neither is there any law of cyclical recurrence or of decadence.

The bulk of Pareto's *Treatise* is devoted to stressing the strength and constancy of what he calls the 'non-logical' elements in human behaviour and to an account of the various ways in which people try to give a flavour of rationality to conduct that is really rooted in feeling and impulse.

His book makes fascinating reading, but it provides no basis for a scientific sociology. The fundamental terms are astonishingly vague. There is no adequate definition of 'instincts', 'sentiments', 'interests' or 'residues' nor of their relations to each other. The 'residues' in particular are so loosely described that it is easy to find the same residue in very different movements of thought or practice. Thus, to take but one example, to find the 'residual' that is to say, the constant and invariable elements in religious manifestations in the 'residue of activity' without further specifying the kinds of activity or considering the intellectual and emotional needs which are at work can hardly be said to constitute a profound contribution to the psychology of religion.

In essentials, Pareto's approach is psychological and not sociological. He does not endeavour to study the social influences affecting belief and behaviour but, on the contrary, finds the explanation of social behaviour in the permanent underlying psychological elements and their varying combinations in different societies. His approach therefore requires a comparative study of individual differences and of the varying distribution of mental traits in different societies. But he makes no effort to establish such a differential psychology, nor does he pay any attention to what psychologists have to say on the analysis of motives.

In brief, Pareto has provided abundant examples of the vagaries of bias, prejudice, self-deception and sophistication, but his analysis of the processes involved lacks precision, and I doubt whether much of it can survive critical scrutiny. In particular, his account is open to the objection that he never questions its fundamental assumptions. He accepts without question the dogma that reason is concerned with means only and has nothing to do with the choice of ends and that value judgements or norms of action are just the expression of 'sentiments'. He is impressed by the fact that in making moral judgements, for example, people are swayed by superstitions and prejudices which deceive both themselves and others. But this applies to all human thought and action and, if seriously pressed, would lead inevitably to the conclusion that there can be no logical thought or action at all. There is in his vast treatise no serious effort to examine the difficulties which stand in the way of collective rational action and the endless misunderstandings, maladjustments and mutual frustration which it has to meet. The result is that he greatly underestimates the role of rational reflection in shaping the lives of individuals and the history of societies.[1]

Marxism or rather, misunderstanding of Marxism, has also contributed to the distrust of reason. This seems to have happened in two ways. The first is connected with the view adopted of the role to be assigned to individual conscious striving in the historical process. 'We make our own history' Engels tells us. 'Nothing occurs without conscious intent . . . yet only seldom does that occur which is willed . . . Out of the conflict of innumerable wills and acts there arises in the social world a situation which is quite analogous to that in the unconscious natural one' (*Feuerbach*. Duncker, ed., p. 56). Elsewhere he adds that historical events may be viewed as the 'product of a force acting as a whole without consciousness or intent'. But this does

---

[1] For further discussion *see* 'The Sociology of Pareto' in my *Reason and Unreason in Society*, ch. iv.

not necessarily involve a denial of the importance of consciously directed action. As Engels explains, from the fact that individuals in interaction produce results which as such were never willed by any one, it does not follow that what individuals contribute equals zero. 'On the contrary every will contributes to the result and is so far included within it' (Letter to Bloch). Engels further explains that the forces at work in society operate blindly only so long as we do not understand them. But as in other fields growing knowledge will enable us to subject social forces to our will, so that the use of them for the attainment of our aims will come to depend entirely upon ourselves. (*Anti-Dühring*, Eng. Trans. p. 307).

There is, however, a certain ambiguity in all this, for the growth of knowledge itself is held to be determined by economic conditions. This brings us to a second source of the distrust of reason, namely the emphasis on 'ideology' that is, the distortion of thought due to class bias, conscious or unconscious. This has been taken by many to rule out all objectivity. Marx himself had no doubt that when class antagonisms have disappeared valid knowledge, untainted by ideology, would become possible. But Marxist exegesis is notoriously controversial. Some would hold that the passage to the classless society involves a radical break, a passage from pre-history to history, and that until this has occurred no objective knowledge is attainable. Others argue that even in the intervening period thought may be more or less objective, in proportion as it is practically useful in bringing about the ends to which the revolution is committed. Others, less friendly, argue that this view of the nature of scientific development and of the society of the future is itself conditioned by the class struggle and may no longer hold when the capitalist system has been overthrown. Other truths would then emerge which would be valid for the societies then formed. Whether objectivity is possible in human affairs or in what degree thus depends on which of these interpretations is adopted. Those who are not in the Marxist fold will agree that knowledge is always 'relative' in the sense that it cannot claim to have reached final or absolute truth, but that it can be more or less objective in proportion as methods are available for avoiding bias and prejudice. In other words, the study of human behaviour necessarily suffers from a certain relativity of outlook and this affects history as well as the social sciences, but in both cases, it admits, in varying measure, of self-correction.

A curious but indirect influence of Marxism is to be seen in the use made of it by some theologians. Thus Niebuhr credits Marxism with having revealed the essential weakness of human nature, erring only in confining the tendency to hide self-interest behind a façade of general interest to the dominant class, while in fact all alike are tainted (*Nature and Destiny of Man*, I. p. 37). The social elements in human nature are not denied. But there is a reluctance to admit genuinely disinterested acts either by individuals or groups, or if allowed, they are not considered historically important. They are reduced to the occasions when there happens to be a coincidence between the interests of the individual and the wider community or between the interests of a particular community and other communities. As in the case of Pareto, who holds a similar view, this despondent attitude is not supported by any comprehensive survey of the achievements or failures of mankind, nor is any method suggested by which such a survey might be attempted. I doubt whether it finds any support in Marxism. Marxism requires no doctrine of original sin. Its underlying assumption is rather that altruistic and selfish motives alike will operate differently in different social structures. Marx himself explicitly repudiated egoistic interpretations of human behaviour and protested against the cynical efforts of those who discern 'behind the cloud of ideas and facts, only petty, envious, intriguing mannikins stringing the whole of things on their little threads' (Cited, Sidney Hook, *Towards the Understanding of Karl Marx*, p. 131).

Niebuhr's view raises the old question of the relations between 'human nature' and social institutions to which already Aristotle drew attention in his criticism of Plato's communism. (Cf. my brief discussion in the chapter on Associations and Institutions, p. 108.) Niebuhr holds that there are defects in human nature so ingrained that they will never be eliminated

B

by a reorganization of society. Changes in social regulations, e.g. changes in the rules of the road, may leave the fundamental stock of human selfishness unaltered, while reducing the occasions which bring it out. On this view improvements in institutions may well have the effect of making men appear better than they are. Likewise it would seem to follow that bad institutions make men appear worse than they are, though this conclusion is not usually drawn. Underlying this view is the belief in 'original' sin, that is, the doctrine that there are in human nature evil impulses which institutions may control, but not eradicate. By contrast, those who think that human nature is somehow better than its performance believe in the fundamental goodness of man. Both views rest on too abstract a conception of human nature; separating it too sharply from its manifestations in behaviour. The concept of an 'original' human nature, good or bad, has little meaning.

The various anti-rationalist trends of thought which I have briefly described owe their influence, I think, not to their inner coherence, but to the fact that they gave expression to a more general disillusionment due to the collapse of the high hopes for speedy progress held out by the humanitarian thinkers of the eighteenth and nineteenth centuries. The two world wars, the horror and savagery of the Nazi period, all the more terrible for its cold and systematic ruthlessness, revealed the weakness of reason in human affairs and raised the question whether we can trust it to save us from the repetition of like or worse disasters. It is now clear that the virtues of popular education and of the machinery of democracy had been vastly overestimated. Educational systems have even now hardly begun to tackle the unconscious forces that stand in the way of rational thought. Even among the most advanced nations they have not been successful in equipping the large majority with a greater capacity for independent judgement, with the power of resisting the tendency to hasty generalization or withstanding the pressure of mass suggestion. As far as higher education is concerned the tendency to excessive specialization has brought with it dangers to which already Comte drew attention, but which are now greater than in his time. The specialisms attract men of the highest ability, whilst the task of co-ordination is left to men not conspicuous for width of knowledge or moral wisdom. Hence advance in special skills is not necessarily reflected in general social policy and even gives rise, as is happening now in the case of atomic physics, to special temptations and dangers which the available social wisdom may not be able to control.

As to democratic institutions no one could write of them now with the Mazzinian enthusiasm. Yet the critics must be reminded of two things. First, totalitarian forms of dictatorship succeeded in establishing themselves only in countries which have had very little experience of democracy. The others not only remained democratic but widened the application of the democratic principle by giving votes to women and by enabling the working-classes for the first time in history to establish parties of great strength. Secondly, democracies on anything like a popular basis have only existed for about, say, 150 years and their achievements during this short period are by no means contemptible. Consider the cautious verdict of Lord Bryce writing in 1921:

'If we look back from the world of today to the world of the sixteenth century, comfort can be found in seeing how many sources of misery have been reduced under the rule of the people and the recognition of the equal rights of all. If it has not brought all the blessings that were expected, it has in some countries destroyed, in others materially diminished, many of the cruelties and terrors, injustices and oppressions that had darkened the souls of men for many generations.'
(Modern Democracies, vol. 2, p. 585.)

Democracy is still faced by three great difficulties. The first is the persistence of great social and economic inequalities. The second is the failure to apply the democratic principle to nationalities and dependencies. For these difficulties solutions are now available, at least in theory, and in recent decades considerable progress has been made in applying them. The third is the most intractable. It arises from the persistence of sovereign independent states and the failure of applying the principle of self-government to the world as a whole. Unless or until these difficulties are solved democracy is a partial principle, haltingly and inconsistently applied, and its failure may be due more to this incompleteness than to its inherent defects.

There are signs, I believe, that the period of disillusionment is over and that increasing attention is being given to the critical evaluation of institutions in the light of principles that can be rationally defended. Both from the side of ethics and psychology it is recognized that the analysis of rational action in terms of a means-end relationship is a crude over-simplification. In many of the higher activities of the mind, intellectual and artistic, process and result cannot be separated. The purpose grows, changes and develops as the activity continues. Even in practical activities the ends change as we proceed to realize them. Reason is thus concerned not merely with the appropriate linking of means and ends, when these are explicitly known, but also with eliciting the ends implicit in behaviour, and clarifying the standards which underlie our orders of preference and the assumptions on which they rest. It follows that if there is such a thing as rationality in action reflection on values and standards must be able to claim validity.

The questions thus raised belong to moral philosophy, but they are of profound importance also for moral psychology. I take the view that with suitable qualifications the tests of rationality in morals are similar to those we employ in estimating the rationality of theoretical knowledge. If this be so, we should be able to use these tests in estimating the degree to which moral beliefs as embodied in institutions are being rationalized. The most important of the criteria are universality, inner coherence and capacity for self-criticism and reconstruction. As regards the first, moral principles are now, in theory, taken to be universal, applicable to all persons coming under them. In practice this is seen (a) in the acceptance by most modern communities of equality before the law, that is, the right of equal protection in respect to all fundamental rights; (b) in the efforts made to secure to individuals not only political, but also social and economic, equity. Judged by this test communities differ greatly, but in all of them arbitrary differentiation or inequality comes increasingly under attack. The most important limitations to universalism are seen in the way states deal with the problem of colour, the rights of nationalities, and above all in their attitude to war. Everywhere we see the beginning of efforts towards a rational solution of the problems thus raised, but the results so far are still a long way from satisfying the demands of a consistent universalism. The most palpable failure of reason is seen in the attitude of states to the threat of war. Everybody recognizes that in an atomic age, war is irrational, but fear and distrust stand in the way of rational discussion. It is clear that short of a radical solution which would make it impossible for states to take the law into their own hands, arguments whether this or that weapon is morally permissible are bound to end in muddle and confusion.

As to inner coherence, no exhaustive examination is needed to show that the working codes of conduct contain a mixture of elements of varying consistency. Witness the mingling of intimidation and correction, retribution and reparation in the penal codes of even advanced societies. There is a similar incoherence in the principles implicit in the regulation of economic relations, or of marriage and the family. The reasons for this lack of coherence are mainly historical. Firstly, moral systems have complex origins. Thus the ideals of a community may be derived from its religion or religions, the moral and legal codes may have different roots and the synthesis of the three may be very imperfect. Secondly, in developed societies the various groups and classes tend to have moralities of their own and these may give rise to conflicting loyalties and obligations. On the whole, however, there is in modern societies a gradual enlargement of the areas within which common standards apply and a growing effort to get rid of contradictions. We may reasonably expect this trend to continue.

Finally, there is the test of capacity for self-criticism and reconstruction. Advance in this direction may be seen not only in the deliberate efforts of philosophers to clarify moral ideas and beliefs, but also in the growing practice of basing legislation on impartial inquiry into the relevant facts and a critical scrutiny of the ends to be pursued. That the recognition of this need has passed from philosophers to jurists and administrators is important evidence of the growing rationalization of public policy.

All this is subject to the overhanging doubt that a third world war may end in the destruction of civilization. On the assumption that statesmen will not be so stupid or helpless as to lead mankind to suicide, we may infer from existing trends that our knowledge of natural forces will continue to grow and that the technical problems involved in supplying the material conditions are not insoluble. On the other hand, in matters of political and social organization the future of rationality as judged by the above criteria is far more uncertain. In the Western world what has so far been achieved in some societies in equalizing rights and removing the barriers that divide men, in reconciling order with freedom and bringing together the principle of personal development with the principle of social responsibility justifies the conclusion that we are beginning to discover the conditions of a rational ordering of life and that with growing knowledge and insight steadier progress may become possible. Whether the communist societies will eventually move in a similar direction no one can predict. It is possible, however, that if the fear of war is eliminated, the spirit of free inquiry will reassert itself and bring about a revival of the moral elements which gave socialism its dynamic quality in its early stages and so strengthen any tendencies that may now exist towards liberalization and humanization.

The waves of irrationalism are, assuredly, far from having spent their force. The greatest danger now lies in the use of reason to defeat reason. But reason is a versatile capacity and it is hard to believe that ultimately it can be self-destructive. It has to be remembered that the rationality of political action depends not only on the rationality of the political leaders but also on the mental structure of the communities on whose behalf they act and of the communities with which they have to come

to terms. Clearly communities differ enormously in the influence public opinion has on policy and in the way in which public
opinion is formed. Even in experienced democracies representative assemblies too often fail in their function of eliciting and
guiding public judgement. This is not surprising in view of the
methods used in selecting representatives, and the complexity of
the problems they have to deal with. The qualities that make for
success are not necessarily those of high intelligence or moral
insight, but a strange and unpredictable blend of the good, bad
and indifferent. In autocracies the blend is even stranger and
more unpredictable. In view of these complexities and the
growing interdependence of the internal and external policy of
states, the question that has to be faced is not so much why
reason has achieved so little in the ordering of social relations
as why anyone ever expected it to achieve more.

Introduction to the Eighth Edition

SPECULATIONS ON SOCIAL and political problems must from
the nature of the case have a psychological basis, conscious or
unconscious. Whether we are concerned with a description or
analysis of the actual behaviour of human beings in the various
spheres of activity, or with the problem of ideals or principles
which man *ought* to follow, a knowledge of human potentialities,
of the nature of his innate and acquired equipments, of the
motive forces of life and conduct is evidently of the greatest
importance. And we do in fact find that writers on Politics,
Economics, Ethics and the like proceed on certain assumptions
as to what are called the 'laws of human nature'. Thus to take
but a few instances, the political theory of Hobbes rests on the
assumption that man is moved to action by fundamentally
egoistic impulses and that the basis of obedience is fear, while
such writers as Sir Henry Maine find that basis in habit and
others again in rational consent. The Utilitarian School in
politics and ethics was based on certain psychological assumptions, though they were not all consciously realized by the
members of that school in an equal degree, viz. that human
action is guided entirely by a conscious pursuit of ends, that the
sole motive of action is the attainment of pleasure and the
avoidance of pain and that happiness is identical with a sum of
pleasures. These or similar psychological assumptions also
underlay the economics of the *laissez-faire* school. Again in
popular thinking on social matters nothing is more common
than a reference to what are supposed to be the laws of human
nature. Human nature being what it is, it is often maintained,
wars are inevitable. Others argue that while human nature
remains the same, Socialism is utterly impracticable and open
competition the only method of securing initiative and energy

in industry. One of the most common dogmas in this connexion
is the immutability of human nature, which is invariably urged
against any new proposals. One would imagine that we were in
fact possessed of a science of human character and conduct
which would enable us to speak with any certainty of what is
and what is not attainable by human endeavour, whereas the
truth is that such a science is yet in its infancy and has hardly
gone beyond the stage of rough empirical generalization.

Despite the obvious importance of a knowledge of the
psychological factors operating in political and social affairs, the
conscious application of psychological principles to social
theory or rather the attempt to build up a social psychology is a
recent growth. The movement may be said to begin in the
latter half of the nineteenth century and is exceedingly complex
No attempt can be made here to disentangle the various elements that contributed to the creation of an atmosphere
favourable to the psychological point of view; but the following
phases may be distinguished.

1. In the first place the philosophy of Hegel, and, in a
different way, the work of Comte, led to the conception of
humanity as a manifestation or expression of a spiritual principle, and in Hegel of the *Volksgeist* or Folk-Soul as an emana-
tion or embodiment of the World-Spirit. This conception of a
national mind or soul was not, however, worked out psychologically, but was essentially a metaphysical conception, though in
Hegel's work there is to be found a good deal of psychological
interest. The Hegelian movement is of importance because it
fitted in with and largely inspired a romantic and mystical
conception of the nation whose influence can be traced in
various directions, in the sphere of literature and art, as well as
in the interpretation of law and language, of myth and custom.
Thus to take but one example, the so-called Historical School
of Jurisprudence founded by Savigny was evidently influenced
by Hegelian conceptions, for according to it law is not the
product of conscious intellect and will, but is a natural growth
or expression of the spirit of a people. This conception of the
national soul, however, remained very vague and hazy, and

cannot be said to have been fruitful of results in the field of historical jurisprudence.

Not unconnected with Hegel was the work of Lazarus and Steinthal, who are usually referred to as the founders of social psychology and who in 1860 established a periodical for the study of Folk Psychology and Philology, in which they laid down a very elaborate programme. Their conception of social psychology is interesting and does not seem in essentials to differ from that of Dr McDougall. 'The duty of Folk Psychology,' says Lazarus, 'is to discover the laws which come into operation wherever the many live and act as one.' Its business is to give a scientific account of the whole life of a people as exemplified in their language, art, religion and conduct, above all, it is to deal with the changes that take place in the minds of peoples, their evolution and decay. The procedure was to be entirely empirical, i.e. based on an examination of the facts of direct observation and of those furnished by ethnology and other sciences of human life. Folk Psychology was to consist of two parts, one dealing with the general principles underlying the phenomena common to all groups or peoples and the other, called by them Psychological Ethnology, dealing with the psychological peculiarities of peoples and groupings. (With this may be compared the following statement of McDougall: 'Group Psychology consists properly of two parts, that which is concerned to discover the most general principles of group life and that which applies these principles to the study of particular kinds and examples of group life.' – 'The Group Mind,' p. 6) It is difficult to estimate the importance of the work of Lazarus and Steinthal. Apart from rather forbidding discussions as to the nature of the social mind (in which they seem to labour under the difficulty of bringing together in one system two radically incompatible theories, viz. the psychology of Herbart and the metaphysics of Hegel), their actual contributions lie rather in the field of detailed philology than in social psychology proper. In any case it is difficult to ascribe to them any influence which can be directly traced.

References may be made also to the very important work of

Wilhelm Wundt, who in Germany is regarded as the most eminent representative of Social Psychology. He conceives of the latter as concerned with the study of the mental products of communities such as language, mythological ideas and customs. Social psychology is thus according to him an integral part of general psychology, or rather a method of study designed to help us in an understanding of the more complex mental processes. His voluminous works on *Völkerpsychologie* are therefore devoted to a study of language, myth, custom, law and social organization from this point of view. In a later and briefer work he has also attempted to give a synthetic view of human development and of the phases through which it may be said to have passed.[1]

2. The work so far discussed falls largely under the first part of Lazarus and Steinthal's programme. But there exists also a large literature on what may be called differential social psychology which deals with the mental characteristics peculiar to different races and peoples. This literature was largely inspired by the remarkable development of national self-consciousness during the nineteenth century. Thus, e.g. the war of 1870 and the desire to determine the cause of the German victory led to the work of Pater Didon, *Les Allemands* (Paris, 1884). Again the frequent prophecy of the decay of the Latin peoples as compared with the Germanic largely inspired Fouillée's *Psychologie du peuple français* (Paris, 1898). To this group belong also the later work of Fouillée. *Esquisse psychologique des peuples européenis*; Leroy-Beaulieu's *L'Empire des Tsars et des Russes*, 1889; Hugo Münsterberg's *The Americans*; Boutmy's *Essai d'une psychologie politique du peuple anglais au XIXme siècle*; Masaryk's *Russia and Europe*; and many others. Mention may also be made of the attempts at race psychology inspired by such writers as Gobineau and Chamberlain.

Many of the books belonging to this group are distinguished by considerable insight into the psychology of peoples, but it is doubtful whether they belong to the sphere of science proper.

---

[1] For a brief account of this later work see an article by the writer in the *Hibbert Journal*, 1916–17, p. 337.

They abound in facile generalizations, based on general impressions and vague assumptions. They all suffer from the fact that as yet we have not a proper science of character and from the absence of any generally accepted methods of record and observation. Generalities such as that one people is given to abstract ideas while another is inductively inclined, or that one people is sceptical and critical while another is ready to accept any dogma, are worth very little. In particular much confusion has arisen from the use of collective terms and from the assumption that there exists a racial or national mind which persists as such and is responsible for what befalls a people; and the result is – hasty generalization, to which the notion of a group mind too easily lends itself. Many of the statements made by different observers with regard to national characteristics contradict one another. Thus, e.g. according to Chamberlain, the Jews are markedly strong-willed, while the Germans are noted for intellect; whilst Lapouge tells us that Homo Europeaus has but an average intellect while his will is strong. Again the explanations that are offered for national characteristics are often of a very doubtful character. This applies in particular to the direct influence of climatic conditions. Thus according to Leger, the influence of the Steppes in Russia is towards autocracy. Unfortunately, according to Laban the steppe produces in the Hungarian not only courage and frankness but also a peculiar love of freedom. So again Leroy-Beaulieu explains the dreamy character of the Russians by reference to the Russian plains; while Laban finds in the Hungarian plains the explanation of the realistic temper of the Hungarian. Instances could be multiplied to prove the precarious character of many of these books on differential folk psychology, judged from the scientific point of view. The whole subject is in need of careful analysis, and of a clearer statement of legitimate problems, and of a generally accepted method of record and observation.

3. The development of the theory of evolution and the growing importance attached to the genetic point of view led to much valuable work in comparative psychology which has an important bearing upon the problems of social psychology.

Thus e.g. the genetic method of Baldwin (*Social and Ethical Interpretations*) 'inquires into the psychological development of the human individual in the earlier stages of growth for light upon his social nature and also upon the social organization in which he bears a part' (p. 2). To this phase belongs also the work of Royce and in some respects that of Dr McDougall, and there can be no doubt that they have helped us to get a clearer idea of the relation between the individual and society and of the processes involved in the attainment of the consciousness of self by the individual.

4. The development of comparative psychology and the increasing attention given to the study of behaviour as contrasted with introspection is partly responsible also for the emergence of a new school of social psychologists who are concerned to bring to light the instinctive, emotional and unconscious factors involved in social life. This school may be said to begin with Bagehot, who emphasized the importance of imitation in the social process. He was followed by Tarde, who worked out an imposing sociological system on this basis and who has been largely followed by the American sociologist Ross. The popular works of Le Bon exemplify the same tendency. The earlier work of Professor Graham Wallas (*Human Nature in Politics*, 1908) was also anti-intellectualist in character and was designed to bring out the importance of such processes as suggestion, imitation, habit, instinct and of unconscious factors generally, in social life. Dr McDougall's *Introduction to Social Psychology* appeared about the same time as Professor Wallas's book. In this work, which has exercised a very great influence in many fields of sociological inquiry, he worked out a theory of the instincts as 'the prime movers' of human life and has sketched the main principles which in his view determine all conduct. In his recent work (*The Group-Mind*, 1920) Dr McDougall uses his former account of the root principles of conduct to explain the behaviour of groups as such, e.g. the loosely organized crowd, the highly organized army and the highest form of the group mind yet reached, the mind, of a nation state. Throughout emphasis is laid upon the instincts

and sentiments, whilst an 'idea alone as intellectual apprehension cannot exert any influence' (p. 170). He does, however, also emphasize, though with doubtful consistency, the importance of the 'intellectual' activities for progress (cf. p. 297 seq.).

5. The remarkable development of psychopathology associated with the names of Freud, Jung and others has also led to important contributions to social theory, tending largely in a similar direction to the work just referred to under our fourth head. The results of psycho-analysis have already been applied, often with remarkable success, to the interpretation of the great personalities of history, as e.g. in Freud's work on Leonardo da Vinci and in studies by American writers on Luther and Lincoln. It seems probable that psycho-analysis will throw light on many phases of social unrest and in particular on the mental history of the great exponents of Anarchism and extreme individualism (compare in this connexion a recent book by Aurel Kolnai, entitled *Psychoanalyse und Soziologie*). The Freudian concept of repression is extremely helpful in dealing with the problems connected with political revolutions, as well as with the problem of economic life and activity. In this latter connexion may be mentioned the work of Mr. Ordway Tead (*Instincts in Industry*) and a very interesting paper in which Professor William F. Ogburn tries to show 'how economic motives are commonly disguised through the operation of such unconscious mechanisms as displacement, symbolism, projection, compensation and rationalization' (*American Economic Review*, Supplement, March 1919). Freud himself has applied the results of psycho-analysis to an interpretation of totemism and of taboos, while others belonging to his school have made studies in the psychology of religion from the point of view of the new psychology. Jung and his followers seem to be following a procedure in some sense opposed to that of Freud. Whilst the latter seeks to apply results obtained in individual psychology to the elucidation of the problems of folk psychology, Jung and his school seek rather to use the material of folk-psychology for their interpretation of the facts of individual psychology. It is yet too early to estimate the value for social theory of all this work,

but there can be no doubt that it has opened out many fascinating lines of inquiry and that it has already resulted in important contributions.[1]

6. The tendency of recent work is thus to emphasize the unconscious and instinctive factors of social life, and many writers have used the results of recent psychology as a basis for an attack against what is called 'the intellectualist' or 'rationalistic' interpretation of social life. Such attacks are often based on misconceptions as to the nature of reason and will or upon too abstract a view of them. There have, however, not been wanting writers who have tried to show the place of reason and of rational purpose in social institutions and movements. Thus, e.g., Professor Graham Wallas in his *Great Society* argues that thought is itself a true natural disposition and 'not merely a subordinate mechanism acting only in obedience to the previous stimulation of one of the simpler instincts' (Ch. X).

Reference must also be made to the various works of Professor L. T. Hobhouse, who has given an account of instinct and intelligence, of the nature of reason and will, and of the meaning of purpose in social evolution, which is not open to the objections raised by the anti-intellectualist school.

It is hardly necessary to say that no attempt can be made in this small book to cover the ground which has just been rapidly reviewed. We shall confine ourselves here to a discussion of certain fundamental problems. An account will be given in the first place of the nature of instinct and of the role of instinct in society. This will enable us to deal with some of the more important theories which have been worked out in recent times, seeking to explain social structure and function in terms of instinct. We shall then deal with the nature of will and reason and their relation to the instincts and impulses. It is hoped to show that both intellectualists and anti-intellectualists are often guilty of a mischievous and misleading separation of the empirical from the rational, and that it is this false separation which is responsible for many of the arguments against reason

[1] On this whole subject see an interesting article by H. E. Barnes on 'Psychology and History' (*American Journal of Psychology*, 1919).

or thought as a vital factor in social life. In the second place, a critical account will be given of the theories as to the nature of the social mind. This discussion might be thought arid and fruitless by many, but unfortunately those who profess to despise such discussions of the nature of the group mind are often the very people who are unconsciously dogmatic about it, and who at any rate in the actual working out of their social psychology use the conception of a social mind without knowing that they are doing so and with disastrous consequences, especially in political philosophy. It has seemed worth while therefore to discuss this conception critically, and to determine whether an intelligible account can be given of it in psychological terms. The result of this analysis is to show that the conception of a social or group mind is of no great value to social theory and that it is fraught with considerable dangers particularly in the sphere of social philosophy. An attempt will therefore be made to give an account of the real facts which people have in mind when they talk of a social mind, in terms which do not imply the latter conception. A discussion will therefore follow of the nature of tradition and custom, of the general will and popular opinion, of the nature of community and of institutions and associations, of racial and national characteristics, and of the kind of unity that belongs to various kinds of social aggregates, e.g. the crowd, the public and the like. In a concluding chapter the bearing of the results of social psychology on the problems of democratic organization will be briefly dealt with.

CHAPTER I

The General Nature of Instinct

THE TERM INSTINCT is still used somewhat loosely in popular and even in psychological literature. But recent investigations have cleared up certain ambiguities and misconceptions. It is now generally recognized that instincts are not absolutely invariable, nor unerring, nor always biologically useful, and there is a general tendency to explain them in biological terms as inherited modes of response to specific stimuli which have been handed down through racial heredity owing to their value in the struggle for existence. It is maintained that out of the random and sporadic acts which characterize the living proto-plasm, certain acts which have proved useful have become established in the race and a basis has been provided for them in the hereditary structure. Accordingly we mean by the term instinctive activity to indicate certain more or less complicated trains of movement which are adapted to certain ends useful to the race, which are congenitally determined, and are independent of previous experience by the individual organism. So far there is general agreement, but difference of opinion still prevails as to the psychical processes involved in or accompanying these trains of movements. To make this point clear it is necessary to discuss the relation between instinct, reflex action, and intelligent action respectively.

Some writers, following in this respect Herbert Spencer, define instinct as compound reflex action. But, as Professor Lloyd Morgan points out, they are essentially different in character. While reflex action is a definite and localized response, instinctive behaviour is the response of the animal as a whole, and what is perhaps more important as a distinguishing feature, it is determined and controlled by a certain craving or want, a special mood or tension of feeling demanding satisfaction and persisting until the whole chain of activity has been completed. An instinct when in action is, that is to say, impulsive in character, it has a conscious side both cognitive and affective. Though, therefore, on the motor side instinctive behaviour may consist merely of a number of reflex acts, yet we can distinguish it from merely reflex behaviour by reference to psychical processes involved in it.

The more difficult problem that confronts us is the relation between instinct and intelligence. It follows from the above arguments that instincts have a conscious side, but are they akin to intelligence? The question is rendered very difficult by the fact that 'pure' cases of instinct are difficult to obtain, especially in the higher animals, and the part played by experience and by heredity is therefore difficult to disentangle. Animal behaviour exhibits varied and persistent effort, and there is no doubt that in some form or another animals do learn by experience. This persistency with varied activity, and clearly the learning by experience must be going on in those very acts. Nevertheless, in character and method instinct and intelligence are distinct. Instinct as such is independent of experience and is often perfect at birth. Intelligent action involves prevision of an end or purpose, but it will be hardly be maintained that this can be the case, for example, in the complicated instincts of insects. The very complexity and marvellous adjustments which certain instinctive acts reveal prove that their purposiveness is only apparent, because judging from the analogy of human experience it could not otherwise be confined to a single series of acts, and animals capable of them would not exhibit what Fabre has called such 'abysmal stupidity', when confronted with a situation for which instinct does not provide.

Though instinct rests entirely on preformed structure, it is yet not mechanical, and though not determined by purpose, it is not altogether independent of it. Indeed, as Professor Hobhouse[1] has clearly shown, it is within the sphere of instinct that

[1] *Mind in Evolution*, ch. vi.

intelligence grows up, and as it develops it decreases the rigidity and fixity of instinctive activity. In pure instincts action is directed to the attainment of certain results by a persistent disposition and the actions are all reflex or sensori-motor. The various stages must be gone through in a prescribed manner which does not admit of any alternative at any stage except within narrow bounds. With nascent intelligence, the intermediate steps become more and more indifferent and the ultimate aim alone of importance. At first intelligence only grasps the ends immediately before it, and if the ordinary means of their attainment fail other means are adopted, whilst in so far as an action is purely instinctive, a disturbance of the ordinary routine would have thwarted the whole procedure. Gradually the sphere of intelligence expands, the power of prevision becomes greater, it comes to grasp further and yet further ends and at last it is capable of grasping the whole purpose of conduct. At this stage, though the ends of conduct may be determined by heredity, the means of their realization will vary enormously with the situation and will be determined by each individual in the light of his own experience. In so far as an action is instinctive then, the successive steps as they present themselves will be taken on the ground of a basic feeling, or 'Stimmung', which gives rise to some vague feeling of uneasiness or distress or want craving for satisfaction, and the steps taken will be hereditary modes of response varying only within narrow limits. The development of intelligence makes the whole procedure more plastic and adaptable, and renders it possible to vary the means for the attainment of given ends, and to use methods very far removed from the stereotyped and mechanical modes of behaviour characteristic of instinctive activity as such.

It follows from the above discussion that every instinct has a conative, cognitive and affective side. There is a perception of the stimulus, a feeling element which may be described as a want or craving or more positively a feeling of interest or worthwhileness, a series of movements and kinetic sensations accompanying them – a feeling of satisfaction in the carrying out or

fulfilment of the action and dissatisfaction with its non-fulfil-
ment. Professor Hobhouse has shown that it is to the interest
element that instinct owes whatever plasticity of adjustment it
possesses. In pure instincts the series of acts which runs its
course under the pressure of this abiding disposition or craving
approaches the purely reflex type. Gradually modifications and
adaptations take place. At first there are merely sensori-motor
acts, involving a vague sense-synthesis, a rudimentary act of
judgement, adapted to the needs of a varying situation, and
finally we reach a stage where obstacles are overcome and difficult situations are dealt with in a manner which can only be
explained by reference to intelligent learning from experience.

The cognitive and affective sides of instinct have been
emphasized by the work of Dr McDougall, and a discussion of
his theory will help us to get a clear idea of the nature of instinct.
Dr McDougall bases his treatment of instinct on the familiar
threefold division of mind into cognitive, conative and affective
tendencies, and he supposes that these elements correspond to
different parts of the nervous system, i.e. the afferent, motor
and central parts respectively. Instinct is, according to him, an
innate conjunction between an affective or feeling disposition,
one or more cognitive dispositions and a conative disposition.
An instinctive activity involves perception of and attention to
certain stimuli, emotional excitement at such perception and an
impulse to act with regard to it in a certain definite prescribed
manner. It is part of Dr McDougall's view that (1) every instinct
has accompanying it an emotional excitement of a particular
quality, though in some cases this emotional excitement does not
possess individual distinctness; and (2) that when the instinct
excited is a principal one, the emotional excitement which is its
affective aspect has a quality which is specific, peculiar to it,
and may be called a 'primary emotion'. (3) Further, according to
Dr McDougall, the afferent and motor elements and therefore
the cognitive and conative sides of our nature are capable of
much modification, while the central part and therefore the
emotional side are permanent and hereditary, and persist unchanged in man. Consequently, in man, the cognitive processes

and the bodily movements of instinctive acts become greatly altered and complicated in the course of experience, whilst the emotional excitement and the accompanying nervous activity remain common to all individuals and are the same in all situations.

Dr McDougall has given the following list of instincts which he regards as principal and fundamental. Each has as an integral and specific part a well-defined 'primary' emotion:

The instinct of flight and the emotion of fear.

The instinct of repulsion and the emotion of disgust.

The instinct of curiosity and the emotion of wonder.

The instinct of pugnacity and the emotion of anger.

The instinct of self-abasement and the emotion of subjection (negative self-feeling).

The instinct of self-assertion (self-display) and the emotion of elation (positive self-feeling).

The Parental instinct and the tender emotion.

These seven instincts with their primary emotions yield all or almost all the commonly recognized emotions. In addition there are other instincts which 'play but a minor part in the genesis of emotions' but have impulses that are of great importance for social life. These include the reproductive instinct, the collecting or acquisitive instinct, the instinct of construction, a number of minor instincts such as those that prompt to crawling and walking. There are in addition some general and non-specific innate tendencies, e.g. sympathy, the tendency to experience a feeling or emotion when we observe the expression of that feeling or emotion in others, suggestibility, the tendency to receive suggestions, the tendency to imitate, the tendency to play, the tendency to form habits.

Instinct is according to Dr McDougall the basis of all human activity. The operations of a well-developed mind are but the instruments for the execution of the impulses supplied by instinct, pleasure and pain serving only as guides and habits acting only in the service of the instincts. 'We may say then that directly or indirectly, the instincts are the prime movers of all human activity; by the conative or impulse force of some instinct (or of some habit derived from an instinct) every train of thought, however cold and passionless it may seem, is borne along towards its end, and every bodily activity is initiated and sustained. . . . Take away these instinctive dispositions with their powerful impulses, and the organism would become incapable of activity of any kind; it would lie inert and motionless like a wonderful clockwork whose mainspring had been removed or a steam-engine whose fire had been drawn' (pp. 42–44).

Dr McDougall has worked out his theory in a highly attractive manner, and his scheme has a certain architectural simplicity which has gained for it many adherents, and it has been used as a working hypothesis in many fields of inquiry with valuable results. It has, however, not escaped criticism, and many of his fundamental points have been called in question. The following points may be noted:

I. The tripartite division of mind into cognitive, conative and affective tendencies seems to be, at any rate in the *Social Psychology*, somewhat too sharply drawn. They are really aspects of a single process. Feeling and conation in particular are closely connected. Thus a feeling of displeasure is an incipient tendency to remove it, a feeling of pleasure is an incipient tendency to preserve it.

II. Further, it may be questioned whether Dr McDougall is justified in regarding an instinct as a conjunction between separate dispositions – structural units as he calls them, i.e. a cognitive disposition and a conative-affective disposition. As Professor Stout has argued, 'this would only be legitimate if it had been clearly shown that every instinctive activity includes the innately determined knowledge of something of the same nature as what is otherwise learned by experience. If, for instance, we could assume that when a young squirrel is confronted with a nut, its innate constitution is such that it knows of the existence of a kernel inside the husk, and if we could assume that every instinctive process essentially involves such innate knowledge, it would perhaps be right to make the existence of a special cognitive disposition part of the definition of instinct.' But all that the facts require is 'the power of knowing or perceiving in general, and a special cognate interest whereby attention is selectively directed to certain objects rather than others'. Dr McDougall does not seem to have proved the existence of special cognitive dispositions as distinct structural units.[1] It is perhaps worth noting in this connexion that Dr McDougall's account creates the impression, no doubt unintentionally, of the instincts as quasi-mechanical aggregates of independent structural units and of the organism as a whole as a sort of bundle of such instincts with their emotions. But it should be remembered that instinctive activity is always the response of the organism as a whole, and the various instincts are, so to speak, predicates having the organism for their subject, ways in which the organism expresses itself or maintains itself. It may be added that the physiological theory that the three elements of an instinct are connected with special parts of the nervous system is only hypothetical.

III. Another important line of criticism against Dr McDougall is that which is directed against his view of the relation between instinct and emotion. That emotions are closely connected with the instincts is now generally recognized, but the peculiarity of Dr McDougall's doctrine is that according to it, the emotion is the affective side of an instinct and that each of the principal instincts has one particular emotion that is specific or peculiar to it. Against this position Mr Shand has put forward some very powerful arguments. It is not easy to do justice to both sides in this dispute because Dr McDougall and Mr Shand employ different phraseology and in a sense they regard the relations of instinct and emotion in reverse ways. According to McDougall, the emotion is part of the active system of the instinct, while Shand thinks that some instincts at least are parts of the entire system of the emotion. This is certainly not a mere question of words, but involves fundamental differences of outlook. Be this as it may, Mr Shand seems to have made good his case as against McDougall in regard to the following points.

1. An instinct may be excited without necessarily involving a

---

[1] Possibly, however, McDougall's 'cognitive disposition' is no more than a disposition to attend and perceive.

specific emotion congenitally determined. It has not been shown, e.g. that nest-building or the pursuit and capture of prey involves a single and exclusive congenitally determined emotion.

2. The same primary emotion may be connected with a plurality of instincts or rather of conative dispositions, e.g. the emotion of fear may give rise to quite different types of behaviour, e.g. flight, concealment, shamming dead, silence or immobility or loudest noise and violent efforts to escape.

3. The same instinct may subserve the ends of different emotions, for instance, the instinct of flight in birds is connected not only with the emotion of fear, but with others, for instance, anger, joy of exercise. The instinct of locomotion serves the emotions of fear, anger, disgust.

Upon the whole, it must be maintained as against Dr McDougall that the affective or 'interest' aspect of an instinct is not, as such, an emotion, but only develops into an emotion under certain conditions, e.g. when there is a delay or check to the impulse or when there is an excess of excitement which action does not satisfy. It is to be noted that when the conative tendency of an instinct is immediately satisfied, the emotional component is at a minimum. The function of emotion seems to be to re-enforce interest and impulse, to maintain the object of the impulse in the focus of attention, to insist upon a satisfying reaction. It is, as Mr Shand says, more plastic than instinct and is aroused when an instinct is not working successfully, or when the action of an instinct fails to satisfy (see Carver, *British Journal of Psychology*, Nov. 1919: 'The Generation and Control of Emotion').

IV. Dr McDougall regards the instincts he enumerates as the prime movers of all human activity, as 'supplying the motive power' to all behaviour. This requires very careful qualification. McDougall's instincts are not really primary elements or unitary principles, but each of them is, as Professor Lloyd Morgan has maintained, a class name comprising many varied modes of behaviour which in a general way serve the same end. When we speak, e.g. of the instinct of self-assertion or subjection, we refer to certain characteristics common to a variety of modes of behaviour, and these terms are simply descriptive class names and not unitary principles which can be regarded as in any way determining these modes of behaviour. It is questionable whether we can rightly speak of the impulses as forces. The impulses are merely the conscious side of certain instinctive processes – a felt measure of the intensity of such processes, but not forces producing them. All that we can mean, therefore, by speaking of the instincts as 'prime movers' is that all the interests in life can be summed up under certain heads, i.e. they are all forms of self-assertion, curiosity, rivalry, etc. But this position too has been seriously challenged by Dr Woodworth. He maintains that each human capacity has its interest side: 'Along with the capacity for music goes the musical interest, along with the capacity for handling numerical relations goes an interest in numbers; along with the capacity for mechanical devices goes the interest in mechanics; and so on through the list of capacities with those that are generally present in all men, and those that are strong only in the exceptional individual' (*Dynamic Psychology*, p. 74).

Dr McDougall's point is apparently that all human interests are to be summed up in the primary instincts and their derivatives, but, as we have seen, the primary instincts themselves are at best but class names comprising many varied forms of response, and it is doubtful whether anything is to be gained by the attempt to derive anything else from them. The whole procedure is really, as I think Professor Lloyd Morgan somewhere says, associationist in tendency. The instincts are more or less fixed modes of response to the stimulus of the environment and in a sense they are all primary, i.e. they arise in adaptation to the environment. May it not be the case that new ends arise for man which are not traceable to the primary instincts? Be this as it may, we must maintain with Professor Woodworth that 'the system of native human motives is much broader and more adequate to the specialization of human behaviour than Mc-Dougall's conception would allow. . . . The world is interesting, not simply because it affords us food and shelter and stimuli for all our primal instincts, but because we contain within ourselves adaptations to many of its objective characteristics and are easily aroused to interesting and satisfying activity in dealing with these characteristics. The field of human motives is as broad as the world that man can deal with and understand' (*Dynamic Psychology*, pp. 75–76).

V. Perhaps the most important objection against Dr Mc-Dougall's view of the place of the instincts in man is that he tends to regard them as self-subsistent and to look at the organism as a whole as a kind of aggregate of them. But in truth, though undoubtedly the basis of human character is hereditary and is to be found in the instincts and emotions, yet the hereditary tendencies do not survive in isolation, but tend to fuse with one another and to be suffused by intelligence. There would seem to be but little evidence to show that the instincts have remained intact and unchanged. Our moods are exceedingly composite and contain the instincts as it were in solution. Often motives which have an instinctive origin do not express themselves by means of the instinctive movements which originally corresponded to the instinct. Our present nature is in other words not a balance between primitive impulses, but involves a new synthesis in which the original form of the impulses may be greatly transformed. A good example of what is intended in this argument is to be found in war. The war-mood is certainly not a mere collection of instincts. No doubt reference can be made to the migratory impulse, the predatory impulse, the impulse of display, the sex motives, the emotion of fear. But all these and others appear in a form highly generalized and fused, forming a kind of new synthesis whose essence appears to be a sort of intoxication and craving for the exercise of power. But war is not merely a recrudescence of the instinct to kill. It is doubtful whether this is an original instinct of man, for the hunting habit appears to be acquired and the nearest relatives of man appear to be social rather than aggressive. What happens is that the war-mood exploits archaic instincts which have survived in us though in a modified form. Human motives are amazingly complex, and can but seldom be traced back to a single instinct which can be claimed to have survived in its original form.

Further in the formation of character, it is not only the individual's inherited tendencies that are of importance. Social tradition supplies the medium in which we act, and determines the methods through which our different hereditary tendencies may find satisfaction. It is, in a sense, a permanent determinant of individual activity and operates in the same way as heredity operates in the life of simpler organisms. Upon the hereditary endowment and the social tradition there supervenes the experience of the individual and the result that emerges is a composite whole in which it is extremely difficult to disentangle the original sources and deal with them as units. We must therefore maintain with Professor Hobhouse that in man there is very little that is pure instinct and that, not only because man is capable of reflexion, of criticism, of bringing the demands of an instinct into relation to the rest of his personality and to the requirements of others, but because his behaviour is but seldom if ever determined by instincts fixed and specific as they may be supposed to have existed, prior to experience and independently of the social tradition. 'Hunger and thirst no doubt are of the nature of instincts, but the methods of satisfying hunger and thirst are acquired by experience or by teaching. Love and the whole family life have an instinctive basis, that is to say, they rest upon tendencies inherited with the brain and nerve structure; but everything that has to do with the satisfaction of these impulses is determined by the experience of the individual, the laws and customs of the society in which he lives, the woman whom he meets, the accidents of their intercourse and so forth' (*Morals in Evolution*, p. 11). The range of behaviour that is summed up under such a term as sexual impulse, or the impulse of self-assertion is extremely wide and no light is thrown upon the problem by referring all that variety of conduct to the uniform operation of a simple instinct. We must look at the individual mind as a whole in relation to his environment, and in that whole the inherited propensities must be regarded as mere potentialities whose fulfilment is supplied by the social environment or by the individual's own experience. 'What is hereditary in man is capacity, propensity, disposition, but the capacities are filled in, the propensities encouraged or checked, the dispositions inhibited or developed by mutual interactions and the pervading influence of the circumambient atmosphere. Elements of true instinct remain, but in a state of dilapidation. Heredity does not operate by itself in human nature but everywhere in interaction with capacity to assimilate, to foresee and to control' (*Mind in Evolution*, p. 105).

From the above discussion the following conclusions emerge:

1. Human behaviour exhibits characteristics which make it historically or biologically continuous with animal behaviour.

2. The basis of human character is largely hereditary. In other words, our interests are largely determined by those basic feelings of tension which constitute the core of the instincts.

3. But (*a*) the hereditary tendencies are not self-subsistent but determine and modify one another so that they appear in man in a fused, truncated and aborted form.

(*b*) While the hereditary basis is permanent, the ways in which the instincts manifest themselves will vary enormously according to circumstances, with the experience of the individual or the social tradition under which he grows up. If we designate the force of tradition, convention, etc., by the term social heredity, and the force of instinct biological heredity, we may say that to explain any particular line of conduct we need to know the precise effect of each of these in interaction with the line of experience of the individual or group of individuals whose conduct is in question.

We are now in a position to discuss the place of the instincts in social theory.

CHAPTER II

Instinct in Society

IN RECENT LITERATURE there is to be noted a marked tendency to explain social phenomena by reference to instincts or impulses. This method of explanation has taken many forms. Some writers – as, e.g. Dr McDougall – base their explanation on the interplay of certain primary instincts such as, e.g. the impulses of self-assertion and self-abasement, the development of altruism by the extension of tender emotion from its primary object, the child, to other persons. Other writers lay stress on some particular instinct as of fundamental importance; thus, Dr Trotter considers the gregarious instinct to be the basis of all social life. Other writers appeal to the pseudo-instincts of imitation, suggestion and sympathy. It will be best to consider these views in the order here indicated, though historically the imitation-suggestion theories take precedence.

1. Dr McDougall finds the basis of social feeling in tender emotion. The latter is the specific emotion which accompanies or is the affective side of the parental instinct. In its origin it was maternal, but like many other characters, it has been transmitted to the other sex, and, what is more important, the protective impulse and the tender emotion, come by extension, to be evoked in us when we see or hear of the ill-treatment of any weak, defenceless creature. Herein McDougall finds the source of all the altruistic emotions. Further, like all impulses, this one, when thwarted or obstructed, evokes the pugnacious or combative impulse with its accompanying emotion of anger. Herein Dr McDougall finds the source of disinterested or moral anger or indignation.

As against this position the following arguments may be

urged. In the first place, as to the social impulses, there is no reason for regarding them as derivative. They arise in the same way as other impulses and have the same biological significance as other impulses, i.e. survival value. They are complex new responses and in all probability not mere expansions of old feelings. In any case they seem to contain elements that differ in kind from family affection, they have no relation to nearness in blood and are more capable of development and transference than the tender emotion that exists between members of the same family.

In the second place, objection may be raised against McDougall's treatment of the whole problem of disinterested action. He seems to think that other-regarding impulses need more explanation than self-regarding ones. But the whole tendency of modern biology and comparative psychology is to regard these two types of impulse as equally fundamental or primary. All impulses we may say are directed upon their objects. The question whether they benefit self or others can only arise at a relatively advanced stage of development, and if we look at the growth of impulses we see that they cannot be entirely egoistic. From the moment in which man becomes a social animal, the most important thing to him is the social life. From the point of view of survival the social instincts are as important as those that relate to the individual. The origin of social action is response to the stimulus of other persons and the nature of this response will vary with varying circumstances and be determined like all other responses by their survival value. The problem of disinterested action is really due to the importation of reflective ideas into primitive action. But if we bear in mind that all impulses are primarily directed upon their objects and not upon the attainment of a good or pleasure for the organism, we may say with Mr Shand that 'Every emotion has a potential disinterestedness, so far as among the stimuli which excite it are some which excite it on behalf of another individual instead of on behalf of oneself.'[1] In any case tender emotion cannot be the root of all disinterested action; for example, a

[1] *Foundations of Character*, p. 49.

moth works for its offspring which it has never seen, nor can
see, and deposits its eggs where the larvae can find protection
and food. Are we, as Mr Shand urges, to attribute tender emotion to the moth? And what can be said with regard to the
developed sentiments, for example, love of knowledge or
beauty? Are they due to tender emotion? The development of
moral conduct involves in McDougall's view not merely tender
emotion and anger or indignation evoked when the protective
impulses are thwarted or obstructed, but also the two primary
instincts of self-assertion and submission. The readiness to
accept the code of one's community, to submit to recognized
authority, to be swayed by public opinion are all in his view due
to the incorporation of negative self-feeling in the self-regarding
sentiment and the attitude that consequently follows of receptivity and willingness to learn by precept and example and be
influenced by the praise and blame of one's superiors. To this is
added the effect of punishment, or later the threat of punishment which brings with it the element of fear and thus comes
to colour our emotional attitude towards authority and to form
an integral element of that complex attitude. To the influence of
authority or power and the impulse of active sympathy which
compels a person to find satisfaction in conduct that pleases
those around him, and to avoid conduct which calls forth their
disapproval is due the gradual moralization of the self-regarding
sentiment. The self-assertive tendencies are, however, not dor-
mant during the process of moralization. On the contrary,
as the individual grows up, he successively throws off the yoke
of those who were once his superiors, and who evoked his
negative self-feeling and finds new superiors in his wider world.
In the majority of cases the social group with its enormous
prestige and weight retains its ascendancy, but there are some
individuals who, when they find by experience that codes are
divergent and that the acts approved in one circle are disap-
proved in others, come to despise the opinions and regard of
the mass of men, to rely on their own personal and moral judgements, to cease to be swayed by the opinion of others and to
attain that stability, self-respect and relative independence which

c

is the highest form of the moral life. Moral advance consists 'in the development of the self-regarding sentiment and in the improvement or refinement of the "gallery" before which we display ourselves, the social circle that is capable of evoking in us this impulse of self-display; and this refinement may be continued until the "gallery" becomes an ideal spectator, or in the last resort, one's own critical self standing as the representative of such spectators'.

With the ethical theory which is implicit in this account of the development of the moral and social life we are not here concerned. There can be no doubt of the great value of much of the detailed description given by Dr McDougall and of the importance of what he calls the self-regarding sentiment. But description is not explanation. To say, e.g. that submission to authority is due to the instinct of submission and negative self-feeling seems to me to be equivalent to saying that people are submissive because they are submissive. The instinct referred to, if instinct it be, is, as has been urged above, merely a class name for a large number of varied modes of behaviour which contain a common element, but these are in no sense explained by being named. Further, the real problem with regard to the instincts in so far as they have a bearing on the social life is the range of their application and the modes of their manifestation. In this case what we want to know is why certain codes grow up in particular societies and command respect and not others, and upon such a problem the mere reference to a perfectly general impulse is of no avail. Further, McDougall's account of the social life, with its emphasis on the instincts of assertion and submission, seems to leave out of account the purely social impulses and the sense of community based on them. McDougall does indeed refer to the gregarious impulse, but this he takes to be a mere impulse to herd together. Is there not also an impulse to act together, to be together?

2. Dr Trotter, unlike Dr McDougall, lays great emphasis on the gregarious impulse. The latter exhibits itself not only in the sensitiveness of each member to the behaviour of his fellows, and in the impulse to be in and always remain with the

herd, but in a profound transformation of the mental make-up of the members of the herd. It tends to make them suggestible to everything that comes to them from the herd, or with the authority of the herd, and its great importance lies therefore in the fact that it gives a kind of instinctive sanction to the opinions, rules, ideals which are developed in a group. It is easy to show that the bulk of opinions which people entertain has no rational basis though they appear to the people that hold them to have a quality of utter convincingness and certainty. Dr Trotter argues that this quality is the result of herd-suggestion, and that even totally false opinions may thus come to possess all the characters of rationally verifiable truth, though in that case the mind may attempt to justify them by a secondary process of 'rationalization'.

The whole system of morality, the power of authority, the influence of conventions and ideals, are all, it is claimed, in the long run due to the influence of the herd. Even conscience is but the sense of the discomfort aroused by the disapproval of the herd, and religion is based on the fact that an individual of a gregarious species can never be truly independent and self-sufficient and hence comes to feel that yearning for completion, for absorption, which is the essence of the religious sentiment.

We cannot here do justice to the brilliant and persuasive arguments urged by Dr Trotter or to the wealth of illustration with which his exposition abounds. It is, however, difficult to resist the feeling, that to a much greater extent than Dr McDougall's account,[1] his work suffers from an over-simplification of the facts. Dr Trotter himself recognizes that the herd instinct is not an instinct of the same kind as, e.g. the instinct of nutrition, reproduction and self-preservation, but is a term used to describe a large number of very different facts. We shall see later that there is reason to believe that suggestibility cannot always be accounted for in terms of the gregarious instinct and involves an appeal to different motives in different circumstances. Be this as it may, one fails to see what explanatory

[1] It should be remembered in particular that McDougall does give weight to all grades of mental development.

value the appeal to the herd-instinct, in so far as it is an instinct, possesses. Why do certain opinions come to possess the prestige of the herd? Differences in suggestibility we are told are due to differences in the degree in which suggestions are identified with the voice of the herd (p. 33). But surely it is these differences in degree that need to be accounted for, and in that respect we are faced with a problem upon which the purely general herd instinct can throw no light whatever.

This line of thought suggests a criticism upon the whole attempt to explain social life solely by reference to certain primary instincts. We have seen above that in man the instincts do not survive in their original definite form, but tend to fuse with one another. It follows that the social life is not a mere balance of instincts but a new product or synthesis in which the original instincts have been greatly transformed. It is therefore a risky procedure to explain social life in terms of any one or any number of the instincts. Moreover, though human conduct and character rest on inherited impulses, the way in which these impulses manifest themselves depends on intelligence and experience and on the social tradition. The latter are therefore all important. For example, when we are told that war is the result of fear or of the aggressive instinct we are really told very little in explanation of any particular war. Antagonisms between peoples no doubt have an instinctive basis, but they are dependent in their particular manifestations upon an enormous complexity of interests, which involves experience and intelligence, though of course they are far from being rational. To account for any particular antagonism, we need to know the history of the peoples, their traditions, their social ideals and institutions, and upon these the purely general instinctive tendencies throw no light at all. Fear, no doubt, is an important factor, as are also sympathy and gregariousness; but the range of application of these emotions and impulses and the modes of their manifestation are indeterminate, capable of expansion or restriction, of being turned in many and varied channels, and the particular direction they take depends on social standards and conventions and institutions, upon habit and training, in short upon the experience of the individual and the race. The real problems of sociology are left unsolved by the writers of the instinct school. It may be of some assistance to be informed that the institution of property has a basis in the collecting or acquisitive instinct, but this tells us nothing of what we really want to know, about the different forms which property assumes in different forms of social organization. So punishment may involve a primitive emotion of resentment, and generally, our moral consciousness, and particularly moral condemnation, contains more elements of primitive impulse than we should like to admit, elements of self-assertion and self-exaltation, elements of aggression and herd-suggestion, and it is a valuable contribution to the understanding of human life to bring their influences to light, but as a complete explanation they are utterly inadequate.

3. *The Suggestion-Imitation Theory of Society.* This theory was first worked out by Bagehot in his *Physics and Politics*, 1873, and was subsequently developed more elaborately by Tarde in his *Lois de l'imitation*, 1896, and from a more psychological point of view by Baldwin. Bagehot thought that imitation was the moulding force of primitive society, and is still the most fundamental of social principles. 'At first a chance predominance makes a model and then invincible attraction, the necessity which rules all but the strongest men to imitate what is before their eyes, and to be what they are expected to be, moulded men by that model.' Bagehot shows that such a process of imitation goes on now in all spheres of life. Fashions in dress, in literary style, in the habits of boarding-schools, even in politics and religion, are due, in his opinion, to the imitation by the masses of some accidental suggestion that happens to 'catch on'. This imitation, according to him, is involuntary and unconscious, and so strong is it that we experience pain when we feel that our imitation has been unsuccessful. 'Most men would rather be accused of wickedness than of *gaucherie*.' In other words, the bad copying of predominant manners is felt to be a disgrace, simply because it is bad imitation.

Bagehot does not give a psychological analysis of the nature

of imitation, beyond saying that it is mainly unconscious and
involuntary, and that 'the main seat of the imitative part of our
nature is our belief'. This shows that under imitation he
included what is now more usually called suggestion. Bagehot
gives many brilliant and interesting illustrations of his theory,
and he does not make the mistake of claiming that imitation is
the only principle of importance in social theory. Imitation, he
shows, is a strong conservative force leading to the acceptance
of stereotyped custom. If we ask how progress is ever made, the
answer is that this is due to another tendency to be noted in all
progressive communities, namely, the tendency to discussion.
The latter encourages originality, gives a premium to intelligence, teaches toleration and independent thinking. In a brilliant
chapter ('The Age of Discussion') Bagehot shows that progress
was made only in those countries that have adopted early the
principle of government by discussion.

Tarde's theory of imitation as the basic principle of social life
appears to have been worked out independently of Bagehot's
Physics and Politics. It forms part of a general philosophical
theory of reality as a whole, and was applied by him with an
amazing fertility of imagination to practically all the fields of
social inquiry. No attempt can be made here to deal with his
theory in detail; and only a brief summary of the main points of
his theory can be given. He finds that the social process consists
in the mental interaction between the members of a group.
This interaction takes three forms, repetition, opposition and
adaptation. These principles are not peculiar to sociology, but
are the 'three keys which science employs to open up the arcana
of the Universe'. They are fundamental aspects of all phenomena. 'Repetition has three forms: undulation, its physical
form, exemplified in the passage of sound waves through an
elastic medium like air; heredity, its biological form, through
which organisms repeat their life from generation to generation;
and last, imitation, its social form, on which society is based.
Similarly opposition has physical, biological and social forms,
the latter including war, competition and discussion' (Davis,
Psychological Interpretations of Society, p. 120). The relative

importance of these three principles is summed up by Tarde in the following passage: 'These three terms constitute a circular series which is capable of proceeding on and on without ceasing. It is through imitative repetition that invention, the fundamental social adaptation, spreads and is strengthened, and tends through the encounter of one of its own imitative rays, with an imitative ray, emanating from some other invention, old or new, either to arouse new struggles, or to yield new and more complex inventions which soon radiate out imitatively in turn, and so on indefinitely. . . . Thus of the three terms compared, the first and third surpass the second in height, depth, importance and possibly also in duration. The only value of the second – opposition – is to provoke a tension of antagonistic forces fitted to arouse inventive genius' (*Social Laws*, 135–7).

In regard to society we may say then that the important processes to which all complex phenomena may be ultimately resolved are imitation (a form of repetition) and invention (adaptation). The essential characteristic of society is imitation transmitting and spreading individual invention. The source of progress is invention, i.e. the adoption of ideas and actions having a new and individual quality. The source of likeness, conformity, co-operation, is imitation, i.e. the adoption of ideas and actions which are replicas of the ideas and actions of others. The social process is a process of the production of similars (contrast Aristotle's 'similars do not make a state'), i.e. a form of relation between minds such that these minds come to be more alike than before, by virtue of their being moulded after a common shape. Inventions involve the formation of new associations. The increase in the power of invention depends upon the increase in the power of perceiving new relations between ideas, of detecting similarities hitherto unnoticed. Tarde seems to think that the range of ability of each nation is relatively fixed and that if an invention requires higher capacity than the people can produce, that people will never make such an invention. The origin of inventions, especially of the higher order and of 'great men' is in part a question of chance. Certain social conditions, however, further inventions, e.g. the number of the population. The greater the number of the population, the larger the chances of higher types appearing. Again, homogeneity of social elements favours both invention and its transmission by imitation. Another important factor is the closeness of social intercourse or communication; the likelihood of invention increases as 'social distance' diminishes.

The social success or the imitation of an invention is dependent upon social causes of two sorts, called by Tarde logical and extra-logical. In the first place, 'logical discord', i.e. non-agreement or contradiction with prevailing views or conventions will make a new idea unacceptable, e.g. a theory violently contradicting the general principles of evolution would not now have much chance of success. In the second place, the extra-logical causes are of three kinds. Firstly, he thinks that imitation proceeds from within outwards, from internals to externals. 'Thus, e.g. in the sixteenth century fashions in dress came into France from Spain. This was because Spanish literature had already been imposed on the French at the time of Spain's pre-eminence. In the seventeenth century, when the preponderance of France was established, French literature ruled over Europe, and subsequently French arts and French fashions made the tour of the world.'[1] Again, dogmas and doctrines are borrowed more readily than rites, systems of law borrow legal principles from one another, before they borrow legal procedure. Herein is to be found the reason, too, why external rites, ceremonies, organizations, are apt to be more archaic than the dogmas, principles or functions they serve.

Secondly, the prestige of an innovator is a factor of great importance. Other things being equal, imitation spreads from the socially superior to the socially inferior. Aristocracies, great cities, successful men, set the tone and the rest follow.

Thirdly, in some states of society, the past exercises an influence of enormous power. Tradition is respected merely because it is tradition. Again, at other times, the novel and foreign possesses prestige. When the new has lost its novelty it becomes a custom itself. 'Ages of custom alternate with those of fashion or mode.'

[1] *Laws of Imitation* pp. 199–213.

Such in bare outline is Tarde's theory. It has exercised a considerable influence on sociological writers, notably on Ross, who has done much to popularize it. The influence of suggestion has been emphasized among others also by Sighele and Le Bon and by Sidis. The latter goes so far as to say that 'suggestibility is the cement of the herd, the very soul of the primitive social group. . . . Man is a social animal, no doubt, but he is social because he is suggestible' (*The Psychology of Suggestion*, p. 310).

It is, I think, now generally recognized that though these theories contain elements of truth, the psychology that lay behind them was defective. Tarde himself uses the term imitation in many senses, and often it is used so vaguely as to cover all forms of inter-communication between minds. In the latter case it is obvious that the statement that 'society is imitation' amounts to no more than the truism that society consists of a number of minds in communication. It is clear that the term imitation needs more analysis before it can be used as a principle of explanation, and in particular it needs to be considered in relation to the allied terms, 'suggestion' and 'sympathy'. Some psychologists regard these three as the motor, cognitive and affective aspects respectively of one process, sometimes called, though not very happily, mental induction. Professor Graham Wallas points out that the same instances are often given to illustrate these rather different processes. Thus, e.g. the spread of fear and flight impulses in panics are used not only as illustrations of the sympathetic induction of the emotions, but also of imitation. The reason is, that panics do in fact exhibit all the three tendencies above referred to; the suggestion of danger is easily communicated, there is a sympathetic induction of the emotion of fear, and an imitation of actions. We may now consider each of these processes in turn.

(*a*) *Imitation.* In Tarde's writings imitation often appears as an unconscious, almost reflex process, and many other writers speak of it as instinctive. A survey of recent comparative psychology, and particularly of animal psychology, shows that under it are really included a number of very different kinds of reaction, belonging to very different levels of mental development.

1. In the first place, by imitation may be meant what some writers describe by the term biological imitation. This is largely unconscious and consists in the copying of the instinctive behaviour of one animal by others, usually of the same species. According to Dr McDougall, 'the behaviour of one animal, upon the excitement of an instinct, immediately evokes similar behaviour in those of his fellows who perceive his expression of excitement. Each of the principal instincts has a perceptual inlet or recipient afferent part, that is adapted to receive and elaborate the sense impressions made by the expression of the same instinct in other animals of the same species. For example, that of the fear instinct has, besides others, a special perceptual inlet that renders it excitable by the sound of the cry of fear, the instinct of pugnacity a perceptual inlet that renders it excitable by the sound of the roar of anger.' In the same way, apparently, according to Dr McDougall, a few other acts, not included in the principal instinct, may act as stimuli, calling forth similar responses in the spectators. It has, however, been disputed whether such a general statement is warranted by the facts. It is clear that in the case of the instinct of pugnacity, the sight of infuriated men *may* evoke wonder rather than the impulse to fight. So the sight of a mother fondling her child does not necessarily evoke similar behaviour in the observers. As Thorndike says: 'They need not be moved to cuddle it, her, one another, their own babies or anything else.' It is also possible in many cases that similarity of behaviour may be due not to direct imitation, but to the action of the same stimulus upon all the spectators, calling forth in each the same instinctive reaction. Again, it may be that the sight of instinctive reaction of others acts as a signal, drawing attention to the object which normally evokes the action. It does not seem safe therefore to lay down a general rule as to the effect of the perception of instinctive behaviour. There are, however, a number of acts, the imitation of which seems to be more or less instinctive, or even reflex. According to Thorndike, they probably include, smiling when

smiled at, laughing when others laugh, yelling, looking at what others look at, listening, running with or after people who are running in the same direction, jabbering and becoming silent, crawling, chasing, attacking and rending, seizing. In all such cases the action imitated is a stimulus which releases in the imitator a train of activity for which he is already prepared by his hereditary structure. It seems to be agreed by most psychologists that there is no general instinct to imitate, but merely that certain instincts, each of which has to be studied separately, have the power of acting as stimuli, evoking similar behaviour in others.

Professor Woodworth points out that some cases that at first look like reflex instances of unconscious imitations cannot really be such. The spectators of a football game may occasionally be seen to make a kick-like movement when, for example, the full back is making a rather deliberate kick. This looks like purely reflex imitation. But very often the movement of the spectator's foot *precedes* that of the player, and cannot in that case be purely imitative. In such cases the behaviour of the spectator depends on an understanding of the situation and on an interest that a certain movement should be performed; for generally the action thus stimulated is on behalf of one's chosen side.

2. In the second place, there would appear to exist a tendency to conform, to be like others. This is noticeable in children, who undoubtedly *like* to imitate, and persists throughout life in various forms. Probably this is a specific differentiation of the gregarious impulse, or at any rate part of the general social impulses, and may be accounted for by the obvious survival value of uniformity of behaviour in emergencies on the part of members of a herd or group. Such imitations, however, are not in detail reflex or instinctive. Intelligence or experience enters into them at every step. They are of importance in such phenomena as the spread of fashions and conventions.

3. In the third place, there is reflective or rational imitation best exemplified on a large scale by the deliberate imitation by the Japanese of European methods and ideas. Many of Tarde's examples clearly belong to this group.

(*b*) *Suggestion*. The term Suggestion is now used for the

cognitive side of imitation, i.e. for the imitation of ideas and beliefs. There is still a great difference of opinion as to the real nature of suggestion and the definitions given of it by various writers are numerous and conflicting. In English writings, however, the basis of discussion has frequently been Dr McDougall's definition, which is as follows: 'Suggestion is a process of communication resulting in the acceptance with conviction of the communicated proposition, independently of the subject's appreciation of any logically adequate grounds for its acceptance.' It is now, I think, generally recognized that suggestibility is not a state of mere passive receptivity, but involves the arousal of some instinctive tendency or of some set or system of ideas which have a strong affective tone, resulting in the inhibition of all conflicting ideas and the forcing of the stream of consciousness in the direction of the ideas belonging to the system of ideas aroused. Suggestibility in other words is due to the evocation of some instinctive or emotional system or complex and the consequent inhibition of conflicting ideas. It is thus not in itself an instinct and depends rather on the operation of other impulsive and emotional systems or complexes.

It is only thus that we can account for the varying degrees of suggestibility exhibited by different individuals and by the same individuals under different circumstances. It follows, as Dr Hart has clearly shown, that to refer any form of behaviour to suggestion in general is not in any sense to give an explanation of that form of behaviour. We require to know in each case the complex of ideas with strong emotional tone to which appeal is made, the particular organization of sentiments and ideals which the individual possesses and whether they are likely to act as encouraging or inhibiting forces. It is true that some explanations of suggestibility have been offered, based on certain specific instincts. Thus according to Dr McDougall the instincts involved are those of self-assertion and subjection; Dr Trotter appeals to the herd instinct and explains all differences of suggestibility as variations due to the differing extent to which suggestions are identified with the voice of the herd; whilst according to others the motive force is generally provided by the sex instinct understood in rather a wide sense. But it seems more reasonable in the light of the available evidence to conclude that different affective-conative factors are involved in different cases. In any case suggestibility certainly varies with and depends upon the degree of organization and sublimation of the instinctive and emotional tendencies of an individual, and such organization involves ideas and ideals and interests of great complexity. Without reference to them the appeal to a general pseudo-instinct called suggestion is therefore well nigh worthless.

(c) *Sympathy*. The notion of sympathy has played an important role in ethics and social theory. Like Suggestion and Imitation, however, the term Sympathy is very ambiguous and covers a variety of facts. In the first place, we mean by sympathy mere contagion of feeling, as when in cheerful society, we feel cheerful. This kind of sympathy is especially characteristic of gregarious animals, and according to Dr McDougall 'it is the cement that binds animal societies together'. McDougall formulates a general law called by him the law of the sympathetic induction of the emotions, according to which the expression of emotion by one person acts as a stimulus which instinctively calls forth the same emotion in the observer. This accounts in particular for the remarkable contagion of anger and fear. It is, however, very doubtful whether there is justification for any such general law as that formulated by Dr McDougall. It is certainly not true that we always experience the same emotion as that which is observed. For example, the observation of fear in a child may induce fear but also a rush of affection. Further, even in those cases where there appears to be direct contagion, it may turn out on close examination that a common cause is acting on the individuals concerned, as when all are affected by the sight of the same object, or that the observer is moved not by a direct sensory stimulus, but indirectly by way of associations based on previous experience.

It is important to notice as Ribot (*Psychology of the Emotions*, pp. 230 seq.) and Dr McDougall (*Social Psychology*, p. 96) have clearly shown that sympathy in this first sense must not be confused with pity, tenderness, benevolence or the like. Sympathy may exist without any tender emotion. Indeed there are many who when they see suffering hasten to withdraw themselves from the scene in order to escape the pain which it sympathetically awakens in them. In the second place, we may mean by sympathy feeling for others as contrasted with feeling as others feel. In this sense sympathy is really not a single emotion at all but a collective name for a group of several altruistic or other-regarding emotions.

It will be seen from the above account that the phenomena comprised under the vague term imitation are of a very wide range and include elements of instinct, habit and reason in various proportions. As to imitation proper, it is much to be doubted whether it is a principle of fundamental importance in the formation of society. It is, however, certainly an instrument for propagating acquired uniformities and so makes for unity. It is thus essentially a conservative factor. Unity or similarity of behaviour are also produced in society by other means by the appeal to common instincts and the inculcation of common ideals. It should be noted also that society depends not only on the 'production of similars' but also and perhaps more fundamentally on differentiation of function. In any case to say that 'society is imitation' is really to include under one term a large variety of very different factors and forms of interaction between individuals ranging from the instinctive to the rational. The phenomena covered by the terms suggestion and sympathy are also of a very wide range and their importance in social life is undoubtedly great. But it appears to be a mistake to regard them as unique factors in the mental and social life. They depend in each case upon different emotional and instinctive tendencies and are hardly instincts themselves. To say that a certain phenomenon is due to suggestion or sympathy in general explains nothing at all.

The Role of Reason and Will[1]

THERE IS AT present a very widespread reaction against what is called 'Intellectualism' and a tendency to emphasize the importance of impulse as against reason, desire and will. In the sphere of belief and knowledge, attention is drawn to the non-rational character of many of our accepted opinions, and to their origin in herd-suggestion and group pressure. In the sphere of conduct it is pointed out that our actions are primarily due to or derive their motive power from the impulses and instincts, while ideas and reason are entirely secondary, incapable of initiating action and confined to the finding of means to ends determined by instinct. This view has received a powerful impetus from recent psychological and philosophical work, but it is important to remember that it is by no means new. We find it clearly formulated in such a writer as Ribot.[2] 'What is fundamental in character,' he says, 'is the instincts, tendencies, impulses, desires and feelings, these and nothing else' (p. 390); and Hume long ago told us that, 'Reason is and ought to be the slave of the passions, and can never pretend to any other office than to serve and obey.' And by passions he meant all the impulsive activities such as appetites, desires and the like, while reason was the faculty of comparing and arranging our ideas and passions, and as such had no motive power.

It is much to be regretted that many of the recent writers who favour this sort of view do not tell us what they understand by

[1] This chapter follows very closely the line of thought pursued by Professor Hobhouse in his *The Rational Good*; it was, however, worked out and practically ready in its present form before the appearance of that work. My argument owes much to Professor Hobhouse's other works and also to the teaching of Professor Dawes Hicks.

[2] *The Psychology of the Emotions*. Eng. Tr. 1897.

reason. They seem to regard reason as a sort of abstract faculty of drawing conclusions from premises and will as a unique activity determined to action by principles different from those that underlie the impulses. As against such abstract views of reason and will, the tendency to emphasize the role of the impulses is perhaps in the right direction; but it is not difficult to see that this anti-intellectualism is really open to much the same sort of objections as the 'intellectualism' which it attacks. Two fallacies generally underlie the arguments of both sides in this controversy: the one may be called the fallacy of separating the empirical from the rational, and the other is a fallacy due to the tendency to break up the personality into distinct units and the failure to regard the self-conscious personality as a whole.

As to the first, it appears natural at first sight to regard the elements of knowledge that are due to sense experience, as something quite distinct from the elements due to the organizing activity of thought. Thus sense and thought come to be looked upon as sharply separated from and even foreign to one another. Sense is that which gives us the data of experience; thought or reason on the other hand is a faculty of comparing and manipulating such data, in the light of principles that it derives mysteriously from its own being or nature. In the theory of knowledge this leads to insuperable difficulties, and in the end to a profound scepticism of the value of thought or reason as an instrument for arriving at the true nature of reality. In truth, however, the contrast is not one of kind, but of degree. From the very beginning of knowledge, sense and thought are inseparably intertwined. Even the most rudimentary act of awareness is essentially an act of discriminating and comparing, correlating. We never do find, in fact, anything that is merely given and not thought or discriminated. The advance in knowledge is made by an extension of this power of discrimination and correlation. General principles are only of value in so far as they do correlate the data of experience. But the empirical and the rational are mutually interdependent. Relatively, we speak of data and the principles that explain them; but the data are not merely given, they already contain elements of thought and reason. On the other hand, the rational has no significance or value except in so far as it does represent a correlation of actual data. 'Sense without thought is blind, and thought without sense is empty.'

So too with regard to will. If we really could remove from will every kind of impulse-feeling, it would have no content whatever and would rule in an empty house. In truth, however, it is just as mistaken to separate impulse from will as it is to separate too sharply sense from thought. On the one hand, in man, even the simplest impulse is modified profoundly by the presence of self-consciousness, and is never a bare impulse; on the other, volition is not a unique and simple activity, but a principle or tendency permeating a body of impulses and desires and giving them unity of direction, and actually consists of, or owes its force to, impulses, desires and feelings.

The second fallacy is closely connected with the first. It consists in regarding the conscious personality as a balance of distinct units each with its own amount of energy. Thus we come to think of the passions and impulses as forces acting upon the personality from without, though strangely enough the personality at the same time consists just of those passions and impulses. Thus, too, we come to conceive of the impulses as subsisting in themselves and as faced with another distinct entity called reason, or will. But surely the conscious personality cannot be thus split up into compartments. Reason, sense, will and impulse are modes of manifestation of the self, ways in which it asserts and maintains itself. The energy involved is the energy of the total self which no doubt takes various forms and finds for itself different channels, according as the activity is impulsive or voluntary, but which remains essentially one. Conflict, of course, there is, but it is a conflict within the self and not between the self and something else outside it. The disharmonies of life are due, in other words, not to the fact that an entity called reason is overcome by other entities called impulses, but rather to the fact that the self has not attained to that degree of harmonization or organization of the impulses which it is the function of the rational impulse operating within them to bring about. Reason and will are not entities distinct from the impulses, but principles working within them and through them, and seeking to canalize the flow of conational energy within well-defined directions, illumined in later phases by clearly grasped ends.

The above argument finds considerable support in recent psychological work. It is, I think, coming to be recognized that will can only be understood as a higher form of conation, which rests on and includes the lower forms, and that development in the sphere of conation goes on *pari passu* with developments in the sphere of cognition. Looking at our problem from the point of view of development or evolution, we may say that corresponding to each level or plane of cognitive development there is a level of conative development. Thus, on the plane of perception, i.e. awareness of objects immediately present to the senses, we have the stage of impulse or instinct. These, as we have seen, have cognitive elements. They may work themselves out by means of sensori-motor acts, which implies a vague sense-synthesis of the total situation to which action is adapted and varied according to requirements. They may even include a vague anticipation of an altered situation, a dim awareness of end or purpose and, of course, they have elements of feeling-tone. So far as there is control of impulse at this stage it is due to these latter elements. Pleasurable feeling-tone tends to reinforce impulse, while painful feeling-tone tends to restrict it, and in animals capable of learning by experience, to modify it or turn it into some special direction, determined largely by the conditions of survival.

On the next level we come to what Professor Stout calls the stage of free ideas, the stage at which the mind can go beyond the present, call up past experience, and on the ground of past experience, perhaps, anticipate the future. On the conative level, we have at this stage the beginnings of purposive action proper, which may be called *desire* and defined best, perhaps, in the language of Professor Hobhouse, as impulse qualified by an idea. Here there is anticipation in idea of an end to be attained. Action is no longer stimulated or guided by present impressions alone, but may find its starting point in ideal representation. It must be obvious, however, that desire is not something distinct from and other than impulse and feeling. On the contrary, it is just impulse guided and directed by ideas.

At this stage it is important to take into account the doctrine of the sentiments as worked out first by Mr Shand and adopted by Dr Stout and Dr McDougall. The impulses and emotions are in themselves complex, but they tend to become organized into systems of greater complexity still, and it is to these systems that the name sentiment has been given. A sentiment is thus a group of emotions clustering round an object, a complex disposition or tendency to experience a large number of different emotions in regard to that object on different occasions. Patriotism is a disposition of this sort, relating to one's country, a tendency to experience the impulses of attack or defence, the emotions of anger or tenderness, according to the situation. The cognitive and conative-affective elements are very intimately linked up in the sentiments, which are, in fact, systems of percepts and ideas to which there have come to be attached strong emotional and instinctive dispositions. Mr Shand points out that by means of the sentiments man comes to form ends for himself other than the purely biological ends of the instincts. 'With every new sentiment that a man acquires, he acquires a new fear. Loving himself, he fears the loss of his reputation, of his wealth or power, or the affection of those that love him, all which are ends of sentiments lacking in the animals. For these new ends man acquires new means. Through fear man has to conceal many things. He has to conceal his evil thoughts and actions. No instinctive or acquired method for the concealment of material things is here of service. He invents a new method of silence, deception or lies.' From the point of view of the present discussion, it is to be noted that the development of a sentiment involves the correlation of various impulses, desires and emotions and their organization round a certain object, and one of the most important tasks of social psychology is to describe how groups or societies come to be objects of such sentiments and to influence the conduct, thought and feelings of their members. The organization of the sentiments themselves into greater unities is obviously only possible at the stage of conception or thought. It implies the consciousness of self as a permanent entity, having continuity and identity, and the capacity for forming general rules of life and of being guided by broad ideals. It is at this stage that we can speak of will proper. It follows that an act of will is not to be conceived as due to a new and unique factor, but as an act that issues from some deep-rooted and massive system of our nature, from a relatively stable system of interests that forms, so to speak, the permanent bent of our personality or self. It follows, too, that the problem often raised whence the will derives the dynamic energy which enables it to overcome momentary impulses, is a self-made problem and is due to the abstract way in which will has been conceived. Will is not a mere idea with no conative energy, but the whole unity or synthesis of our conative nature. It is essentially a principle of integration, an effort towards harmony, working within and through complex systems of conative-affective interests, and its energy is the energy of our whole personality. In will, therefore, conation and cognition are very closely linked. Borrowing a phrase from Professor Stout, we may say that 'cognition gives the process its determinate character; without conation there would be no process to have a character.' In other words, impulse and feelings are at the bottom of voluntary action, but these impulses and feelings are harmonized or synthesized and given a particular direction by ideas and ideals, by the power of forming comprehensive purposes. An act of will is thus one which issues from the total personality or self, which expresses the deeply rooted interests that form our character, and the unity or degree of integration which any individual has attained depends upon whether he has succeeded in discovering some unifying principle of action that is capable of giving meaning to his life, some wide and far-reaching purpose which harmonizes all his impulses and finds a place for all his interests. It goes without saying that it depends also on the kind of society and social institutions in which he lives and the extent to which that society has been able to

discover the lines of harmonious development for the members
that constitute it. The role of the self in volition, which is
emphasized so much in recent psychological literature, should
be clear from the above account, for the will is just the total
self in action. Some writers, however, speak of the *idea* of the
self as the decisive factor. To this Dr McDougall objects on the
ground that the mere idea of the self can have no conative
value, and he comes to the conclusion it is the self-regarding
sentiment that intervenes in volition and that sentiment forms in
his view the basis and condition of all moral development. It
would seem, however, that what is involved in volition is not so
much, or is not necessarily the *idea* of the self, but rather the
system of dispositions which is the self, and that of course has
conative energy. No doubt the self-regarding sentiment is of
great importance as a correlating principle, but the unity attained through it may be very narrow and unsympathetic. We
could hardly admire the person who does good in order that he
may be pleased with himself. Greater unity is attained by devotion or strong emotional attachment to large ends, and these
ends must be of value in themselves, and not derive their value
from the fact that they satisfy the instinct of self-assertion. This
point, however, has already been discussed,[1] and perhaps need
not here be elaborated.

We may say, then, that the role of reason on its practical side
is not exhausted in the elaboration of means to ends. Its function
is that of harmonizing the impulses by subordinating them to
broad and coherent ends. It has thus the important function
of directing and organizing. We may conceive of it as a principle
of growth and integration, an effort towards harmony. In the
early phases of mental evolution, the synthesis effected is but
small and restricted. The instincts, perhaps, are the first step
to general control, but they are only imperfectly organized.
The rational impulse is first clearly seen when we reach the stage
of purpose proper and of self-consciousness. Both on the side of
knowledge and of conduct, it is an impulse towards system or
integration. In the world of theory reason tries to connect the

[1] See above, pp. 8, 9, 10.

isolated elements of experience and to discover their grounds in some unifying principle. In the sphere of practice, reason seeks to form life into a harmonious whole. It is a mistake, however, to imagine that reason starts with abstract principles which it seeks to impose upon the data of experience. The principles are only of value in so far as they grow out of and give meaning to those data. So, too, will, or reason in its practical aspect, is not an entity which interferes in the case of conflict and issues orders based on abstract principles which it somehow derives from its own nature, but is essentially a synthesis of the impulses in the light of principles and ends which find a response in the depths of our nature. Those who argue against reason and will, therefore, conceive of them in too abstract a fashion. The facts which they have in mind are due not to a conflict between an entity called reason and other entities called impulses. The real trouble is that the degree of unity and integration attained by man in society is still but small. It follows that what is wanted is not less but more reason, more knowledge of the conditions of harmonious developments for the individual and society.

Coming now to the role of reason and will in social affairs, the problem usually presents itself at first sight as a problem of the relation between theory and practice in social movements. Now this is a question that cannot be settled on general psychological grounds. No doubt some social theories are but a pale reflection of widely prevalent impulsive tendencies, and others again are 'rationalizations' of powerful emotional dispositions, the real nature of which is but dimly understood. On the other hand, some theories seem to have had real directive value and force, in that they rendered articulate, and gave definite form to, a mass of incoherent impulses and ideas, which without the organizing activity of thought would have remained ineffective and futile. It is quite arguable, for example, that the influence of the French Encyclopaedists was of this character, and undoubtedly the theories of democracy, of socialism, etc., have been of tremendous influence. Very often a single phrase, e.g. 'workers of the world unite', 'a war to end war', manages to sum up a mass of feeling, thought and impulse, and to obtain a response which is perfectly amazing. The place of theory, then, is a matter for detailed sociological investigation, and each case must be dealt with on its own merits.

The problem of the place of reason in society goes, however, much deeper than is indicated in the line of investigation just hinted at. The rational impulse is not in all its stages conscious of itself. It is essentially, as we have seen, an effort towards harmony or integration and is operative long before the stage of self-conscious theorizing. It may, therefore, be that social institutions do embody such a principle of unity, even though they have not always, or perhaps ever, attained the stage of conscious control of the conditions of their development. It may be, too, that their rational character will become more obvious when they have reached that critical turning point in their career. At any rate it does not seem difficult to show that social institutions do represent an effort towards a unitary life, an experiment at harmony, and detailed sociological investigation would perhaps show that this effort is steadily, though not continuously, widening in scope and comprehensiveness. The functions of institutions, considered from the point of view of social philosophy, i.e. from the point of view of what *they ought to be*, is to discover the lines of harmonious development of personality and the methods for securing the conditions necessary for that development. But the 'ought' must not be confused with the 'is', and a survey of social institutions as they are and have been will impress upon us the warning not to exaggerate the degree of rational unity attained by humanity. Social institutions are not the result of any one mind, nor do they generally embody clearly-thought-out purposes. They appear to be rather of the nature of 'trial and error' experiments, groping attempts at finding solutions for the problems and disharmonies of life. The purposes which they embody are very often conflicting, and the degree of unity which they do attain is often won at the expense of suppressing the most vital demands of a vast proportion of the population. A full answer to the question before us would, it must be evident, necessitate a detailed examination of all social institutions with a view to determine the purposes for which they exist, the extent to which they render a harmonious and full life possible, and whether the instruments which they employ are not in themselves oppressive. Such an inquiry, needless to say, cannot here be undertaken. The general nature of social institutions is to be discussed more fully in the sequel, but enough will perhaps have been said to show, that if we do not wrongly conceive of thought as a bare abstract faculty, we must grant that its role in social affairs is of the greatest significance. 'The power of thought, in the long run,' says Bertrand Russell, 'is greater than any other human power. . . . The right kind of thought is rare and difficult, but not impotent.' In any case, we clearly have no right to jump from the argument that institutions are not as rational as they pretend, to the conclusion that the appeal to reason is futile. On the contrary, our business is clearly, constantly to criticize our institutions, to reveal the elements of conflict and disharmony that they embody, and to remould them in the light of rational principles, based on an adequate knowledge of the conditions necessary for a full and harmonious life.

Our discussion has so far been based on an analysis of instinct, will and reason as we observe them in the individual. We are, however, now confronted with the problem whether in social aggregates there develops a mind or mental system which, though made up ultimately of individual minds, is yet different from them or transcends them, and whether it obeys discoverable laws of its own. It is obvious that our view as to the place of reason, will and purpose in society is bound, in the long run, to be affected by the conclusion we arrive at in regard to the nature of the social mind and the kindred problem of the kind of unity that belongs to social aggregates. We therefore turn now to a discussion of these problems.

CHAPTER IV

The Theory of a Social or Group Mind

THE PROBLEM OF the nature of social groupings has been approached from two sharply contrasted points of view. On the one hand, one group of thinkers tends to explain the character of a social aggregate by reference to the essential characteristics of its constituent units, their interactions and particular modes of combination. On the other hand, a group of other thinkers urge that so far from our being able to explain the nature of a group by reference to the individuals composing it, the latter can only be understood through their social group. The individual, it is maintained, owes his very nature to the social *milieu* in which he grows up, and the qualities of any particular social grouping are determined by the conditions of its life as a whole, its history and its relation to other groupings (Durkheim, Gumplowicz).

Both these views are obviously open to serious objection. The first view conceives of the individual in too abstract a fashion and ignores the very important fact that as soon as a group acquires a certain permanence, and develops regular and sanctioned institutions and a tradition, it acquires a certain character of its own which moulds the activities and influences the feelings and ideas of individuals, in relation to whom it may therefore be said, to some extent, to possess a life and character of its own. Again the second view, though it contains a large element of truth, has often been stated in a manner which tends to belittle individuality, and is moreover open to the objection that, so far, no coherent and self-consistent account has been offered of the way in which the unity of social groupings is to be conceived. But, in truth, the opposition thus outlined is a false opposition and is based on an abstract view of the nature of the individual and of society. The unity which belongs to a social aggregate cannot be accounted for by the nature of the units, because the units have no existence at all, out of relation to their social grouping. There are not at first individuals and then a social unit, as there might be bricks and then a pile of them. The relations that bind individuals together are intrinsic, actually constitutive of the individual. But if the individualist view is defective, the strength of the opposed position lies rather in what it rejects than in the positive account it offers of the individual and society. Though individuals are nothing apart from society, or rather the development of individuality is at the same time a development of sociality, yet society is nothing but individuals in relation, and in individuals there is a core of being which is unique and incommunicable.

From the controversies between the opposed schools we do learn at any rate this much, that individuals are intrinsically and essentially related to one another, and that society is not an artificial product, a mere mechanical contrivance to hold together a mass of individuals conceived as capable of existing in the fullness of their being in isolation. It is also easy to see that the relations that hold them together are essentially mental in character, dependent on ideas, feelings, desires, sentiments, purposes. Can we, therefore, speak of society as a social mind? To many people this will appear merely a question of words, and there would be no objection to the use of such terms, if they were clearly understood to indicate a sort of collective and not a substantive unity, and if it were remembered that the whole constituted by individuals in inter-relation is not more real or more valuable than just these individuals in interaction. But it is easy to show from the history of the controversies that have raged round this problem that the use of the term social mind is exceedingly dangerous, or carries with it implications of far-reaching importance. In the first place, the use of the term

Mind or Person to designate society has led to the ascription to the latter of a fictitious unity which it does not possess, to the consequent belittlement of individuality and of minor groupings and to a mischievous antithesis between the good of society and the good of individuals. No doubt the upholders of the theory of the social mind admit and insist that the latter has existence only in the minds of the individuals constituting society, but in the actual working out of these theories we frequently find that the individual is merged and fused in the whole, though of that whole, strangely enough, very little can be asserted that we know to belong to personal individual minds. What is perhaps more remarkable still is that the merging of individuals in the social whole, and the personification of that whole, to which theories of the social mind are prone, often leads to the erection of a dangerous contrast between the good of the whole and the good of all individuals that constitute it. It is imagined then that some proposed action may be for the good of society as opposed to that of its component members. But this surely is mischievous and misleading. There is no virtue in mere collectivity or even wholeness. [All values are values for persons, and the good of the whole, like any other good, must be a good for persons, must consist in something intrinsic to personality, in something that enhances individuality and serves to actualize some human potentiality] Of the good we may say, as Aristotle said of happiness, that if individuals do not attain it, neither does the whole. This does not imply that the things held valuable by a nation, its culture and institutions, are not more permanent than the individuals of any one generation. Of course they are. But this culture and these institutions are in themselves nothing except as sustained and re-interpreted by individuals from generation to generation. The good of the whole cannot be something distinct from and opposed to the good of the members who in successive generations constitute that whole: and history shows that whenever this distinction has been sharply drawn, it was in order to make demands and claim sacrifices from the people, which a reference to real personal values would not have justified.

In the second place, the theory of a social mind affords autocracy or aristocracy the means of coming before us in the guise of democracy. The social mind, though superior and infallible, cannot speak for itself. The great God needs a prophet and an interpreter, but the interpreter *ex hypothesi* claims to express the mind of the people. Thus Rousseau's 'Moi Commun' needs a wise legislator to disclose to us what the will of the people is; and even Dr McDougall, who repudiates the conception of a collective consciousness, nevertheless maintains that public opinion, a wise and infallible guide, is best interpreted by the best minds of the people, and apparently it is the best minds that decide that they are the best. So, too, the kindred doctrine of a real will which is no one's actual will is essentially aristocratic; for 'the true inwardness of our own will' is apparently what the enlightened few tell us it ought to be. In this manner the particular form of government that happens to exist is made sacrosanct and any amount of interference with the individual is justified, on the ground that that interference is merely 'forcing him to be free', is really what he himself wants.

In the third place, the theory of a social mind often leads, as will already have been gathered, to a deification of society and to the ascription to it of a dignity and power above the moral law which binds individuals. It is one of the ironies of these theories that society or even the state is made out to be both super-individual and sub-individual. It is the embodiment of the highest expression of spirit, yet the accepted standards of personal and spiritual values are not applicable to it.

Fourthly, such deification leads to a fundamental and profound conservatism and a tendency to justify the *status quo*. Once we begin with the conception of a mind immensely superior to the individual mind, a mind, moreover, frequently presumed from the outset to be rational, there cannot but follow, inevitably though often unconsciously, an attitude towards it of submission and even adoration, and a consequent disinclination on the part of the individual to put himself against this god. This fundamental conservatism is apparent in all the followers of Hegel, particularly in their treatment of the problem of resistance (except T. H. Green) and is obvious also in Dr McDougall.

For these reasons it is important to examine the psychological foundations of the theories of the social mind, and to determine whether they really help us to understand the nature of community and of the individual.

It is to be regretted that the problem of the nature of social unity has not been approached more empirically or inductively, by a classification and description of the different types of social aggregates. It is obvious that the degree of unity attained and the factors upon which such unity rests in different social aggregates, vary enormously, and an analysis of these different factors would have prevented facile generalization. Generally, the theory of a social mind has been worked out in reference to the large and complicated aggregates such as nation-states, and this fact has, I think, added to the difficulty of the problem. Broadly speaking, there are two types of theory. According to the first, exemplified best perhaps by thinkers like Espinas and Durkheim, society actually constitutes a collective consciousness in which the mental processes of individuals are fused and compounded. A more careful form of this doctrine is to be found in Wundt, who, though he finds room for the individual and for minor unities within society, nevertheless believes that there is a sort of 'creative synthesis' which results in the development of a social mind and will transcending the mind and will of individuals. All such doctrines are helped greatly by the fact that they have discarded the belief in the existence of a soul-substance, but conceive of the self simply as a series of mental processes exhibiting a certain continuity. Such continuity, they hold, can also be shown to exist in collective mental phenomena.

The second type of theory, represented largely by the German Idealists and their followers in England, and worked out by the latter in particular in connection with the doctrine of the general will, is based not so much upon fusion or compounding of the mental processes of individuals in society, but rather upon the essentially social character of mental contents. It is maintained that the individual self actually consists of, owes his very nature to, his relations to others, that the ideas and beliefs which he entertains, the purposes after which he aims, are social products, that his character is moulded by the social *milieu* in which he lives. Writers of this school generally repudiate the belief in an actual collective consciousness; but in the working out of their theory, it will generally be found, that surreptitiously and perhaps unconsciously, a transition is made from unity of content to unity of existence and process; and in such cases it becomes difficult to distinguish this type of theory from the first. Dr McDougall's theory, as worked out in his *Group Mind*, occupies an intermediate position between these two types of theory. In this chapter it is proposed to discuss the theories of Espinas, Durkheim and McDougall. The problem of the general will is reserved for a later treatment.

1. According to Espinas,[1] society is or possesses a collective consciousness, a 'conscience multiple'. Ideas and traditions mingle, and thus a process of communication between soul and soul is brought about, which results in a real *fusion de consciences multiples en une seule*.

The peculiar attachment which members of the same group feel for one another would, he thinks, be inexplicable, if the self of each did not include and embrace that of all the others. Consciousness is not an absolute, indivisible thing, but a reality capable of diffusion and division. The two essential constituents of consciousness, presentations and impulses are in the highest degree communicable. Perceptions pass, by means of signs, from one consciousness to another, and emotions and impulses spread instantaneously at the beck or sign of a leader, and the energy of these emotions is in direct proportion to the numbers of the members and the organic cohesion of the society. Thought in general and the impulses illumined by it are, Espinas thinks, like the forces of nature, susceptible of diffusion, division and transmission, of existing in a state of potentiality at times, and at others becoming active through concentration. The self of a person no doubt contains something more than these communicable modifications, but this something is not the mystical sub-

[1] *Des Sociétés Animales.*

stance of the schoolmen, but consists rather of a background of ideas and unconscious tendencies, which under various hereditary influences and external conditions, have taken in each individual a particular form or turn, and of the organic structure itself, which under conditions peculiar to each individual has been determined in a particular way. But this background is not something that really separates one individual from another, because the instinctive tendencies and the organic structure of individuals, though incommunicable directly, are essentially racial in character and undergo change and development determined by racial factors. Further, society has a reality of its own, for one ultimate criterion of reality is coherence and consistency, and social phenomena are regular and conform to law; another criterion is existence-for-self, and society is aware of itself. 'It is a consciousness existing in itself and for itself.'

I have dealt especially with this doctrine of Espinas because it exhibits clearly and unambiguously one of the confusions which lie at the root of most of the theories of the social mind. Recent discussions, both in psychology and epistemology, have brought out the importance of distinguishing clearly between acts or processes of consciousness and what have been called contents (Inhalte). The tendency, I think, is to confine the term mental or psychical to the processes, to the experiencing as distinguished from what is experienced. It follows that psychical or mental character belongs only to the immediate experiencing of individuals at the moment of their experiencing. Contents on the other hand are not mental, not structurally or fundamentally part of the mind. Espinas hopelessly confuses process and content. In one place he speaks of mental *operations* passing over by means of external signs into the intelligence of others who are present, whilst elsewhere he speaks of ideas or presentations as passing over into other minds. What is it that passes over, the process or the content? The phenomena observable in crowds need no such assumption as that of an actual fusion of mental processes. Mental processes can only be individual, but some of them are qualified in a particular way by a particular environment, in this case the presence of a mass of people. When a mob is urged by fear or anger it is surely not the same fear or anger which they all experience. What happens is that in a crowd each individual becomes more suggestible, more imitative, less responsible and critical, but the processes of limitation, sympathy and the like are surely still individual processes.

Again, we may ask whether Espinas' second criterion of reality is satisfied. Are societies conscious of themselves? If they are, why is it so difficult to determine what the social mind thinks? It is, I think, very remarkable that while writers on social psychology so frequently point to the communicability of minds, novelists and other observers of human nature are struck with the isolation and distance between different minds, with the cross-purposes or misunderstandings that prevail. No doubt men share in common spiritual possessions, but these belong to the sphere of contents and values and not to processes or functions, and in so far as they are actually experienced by different individuals they are different and peculiar in each case.

We must, as Simmel[1] has clearly shown, distinguish between the concrete mental processes in and through which custom, myth or language arise, and their ideal content as such. The principles of law or the rules of grammar are not processes occurring in individual minds, though they can only be apprehended through such processes.

2. Durkheim's theory of the social mind is based on a distinction between what he calls individual representations and collective representations. There is, in his view, no need to assume an underlying soul or substance. The mental life is made up of a stream of representations, individual and collective.

The primary basis of the individual consciousness is to be found in sensations. The latter are the product of many cerebral cells in interaction, but this product is something new, a synthesis *sui generis*, in which the elements are transformed by the very fact of their fusion. Durkheim notes that a sensation is the product not of a single cell but of several in mutual interaction. Sensations thus produced may be further compounded

[1] Uber das Wesen der Sozialpsychologie, *Archiv für Sozialwissenschaften*, Bd. 26, p. 285.

to give rise to images, and these in turn to individual representations, and the process may be continued further. Just as individual presentations have for their substratum various cells in mutual relation, so collective presentations have for their substratum the assemblage of individuals in society. The latter constitutes a collective soul or consciousness, a further synthesis *sui generis*, and it arises through the fusion and union of individual consciousnesses, ultimately, i.e. through the fusion or compounding of individual representations. 'Collective representations are the result of an immense co-operation which stretches out not only into space, but into time as well; to make them, a multitude of minds have associated, united and combined their ideas and sentiments; for them long generations have accumulated their experience and knowledge. A special intellectual activity is therefore concentrated in them which is infinitely richer and more complex than that of the individual.' Presentations on this view are regarded as having an independent existence, a certain freedom from their substratum. They are partly autonomous and they have the power of mutual attraction and repulsion, of forming all sorts of synthesis determined by their natural affinities and always by the social structure. Durkheim claims that collective presentations have certain peculiar characteristics. In the first place, they are exterior to the individual consciousness. The individual can contain only a *parcelle* of the social mind. Science, for instance, is the product of a vast co-operation, and exceeds anything that can be contained in any individual mind. Religious ideas come to the individual from without and have a certain independence. So also social movements or 'currents' such as those that drive individuals to suicide, are outside any individual consciousness.

In the second place, collective presentations differ in kind from individual presentations. 'The group thinks, acts, feels quite differently than its members would, were they isolated.' Aggregation thus leads to the production of a new being, a psychical individuality *sui generis*, whose presentations have a content different from that of individual presentations. Further, each group has its characteristic forms, with its different habits,

D

needs, which vary according to the numbers of its members, their disposition over the surface of the territory, the nature and number of the ways of communication.

In the third place, Durkheim claims for the social mind a superiority over the individual mind. The collective consciousness, he thinks, is the highest form of psychic life, since it is a consciousness of consciousnesses. It is morally superior to the individual, and is indeed the true object of religious adoration. God is society apotheosized; 'society is the real god.'

Both in regard to content and form the individual mind is indebted to society or to the social mind. It is difficult to obtain from Durkheim a precise statement as to what exactly constitutes the content of individual presentations. Apparently they consist of experiences relating to the body. For all else the individual is indebted to the social *milieu*. As to form, Durkheim claims that all the categories which the mind employs, such as time, space, quantity, causality, are of social origin. 'The categories are the different aspects of the social being; the category of class was at first indistinct from the concept of the human group; it is the rhythm of social life which is at the basis of the category of time; the territory occupied by the society furnished the material for the category of space; it is the collective force which was the prototype of the concept of efficient force, an essential element in the category of causality' (V.R. 440).

In Durkheim's use of the term Representation there lurks a similar ambiguity to that to which attention has already been drawn in our discussion of Espinas. By presentation may be meant the act or process of awareness, or the content which and in and through that process we are aware of. In what sense an act of consciousness on the part of an individual mind may be said to be the product of a union or fusion of more elementary states than itself it is difficult to determine. Durkheim seems to be following the view of the compounding of states of consciousness which we may also find in Wundt. But whether there be such a fusion in the case of the individual mind or not, what evidence is there to show that it can take place between individual minds? . . . *Prima facie* there is no continuity of substratum in the latter case at all analogous to the physical continuity of cerebral cells in the brain of an individual, and empirical evidence of fusion is not given. The truth seems to be that when a fusion or compounding is spoken of, the reference is really to contents. To the latter is then ascribed an independent existence and a power of entering into combination determined by their affinities. This raises a metaphysical question as to the status of contents which cannot here be discussed. I am inclined to take the view of Professor Dawes Hicks[1] that to such contents we are not entitled to ascribe an existence independent of the act of presentation, and to talk of them as fusing is meaningless: it is doubtful, therefore, whether the conception of interaction between minds has any validity. No doubt minds are interdependent, influenced by the activities of other minds, but the influence is of an indirect character. Through speech or other symbolic communication, one mind may be made to re-think the ideas of other people in the present or past, or to accept the ideals and purposes of others and be induced to work with them for their realization. But such common ideas or purposes do not necessitate a fusion of minds. Perhaps such terms as fusion or interaction have really no meaning at all when applied to minds.

Another and perhaps equally fundamental objection to Durkheim's view is that, if consistently applied, it leads to the complete disappearance of the individual and his absorption in the social mind. Apparently the individual mind consists of 'all the mental states which are related only to ourselves and to the events of our personal life' (R.M. xl. 46). But surely even the knowledge of ourselves is dependent on social factors, and even the states of mind relating to our bodily organism rest on sense perception, which again is thoroughly social in character in the sense that it is dependent on memories and inferences due to the teaching and general influence of others. It follows that strictly there can be no such thing as individual representations, and therefore no individual minds, and this is indeed a view to which Durkheim is unconsciously led. Differences of individuality are

[1] See 'The Basis of Critical Realism'. *Proceedings of the Aristotelian Society*, 1916–17.

simply due to differences of bodily feeling. The mind is simply the collective consciousness incarnated in the individual body. 'As bodies are distinct from each other, and as they occupy different points of space and time, each of them forms a special centre about which the collective representations reflect and colour themselves differently.' In any case, to the individual is denied any power of origination. This is the result of a hypostatization of contents and neglect of looking at the mind from the point of view of process and function. Contents may be universal in character, but processes never can be anything but individual. If you and I are thinking of the same object or seeking to attain the same common purpose we do not, therefore, cease to be separate individuals. As regards the categories, too, Durkheim's view is beset with two fundamental difficulties. In the first place, his account of the way in which the categories come to be used on the basis of social analogies seems to me to beg the whole question. The categories are already involved in our ideas of society and to say that their application is extended to other entities thus leaves the fundamental question as to their origin unsolved. In the second place, it would seem that the root of the difficulty is to be found in the fact that Durkheim regards the categories as concepts or general ideas, which leads him to emphasize their social origin, while if we look at them as functional principles, as ways in which the mind organizes its experience, there is no difficulty in conceiving of them as essentially part of the structure of the individual mind.

As to the differences of content between collective and individual presentations, Durkheim is exceedingly vague, as would be expected from the difficulty just discussed of finding a place at all for individual presentations. The fact that individuals behave otherwise in a group than in isolation, does not prove at all that a new mind has arisen through mere aggregation. Special conditions are operative in groups, such as mobs and crowds on the one hand and organized bodies on the other, which fully account for the difference. Thus in an unorganized crowd individuals become among other things more suggestible, while in organized bodies there exists the machinery for collective deliberation and interchange of views. The results that emerge in both these cases differ from one another and from the results of individuals deliberating in isolation. But surely the phenomena referred to do not need a super-individual mind to explain them.

Finally, as to the superiority which Durkheim and others claim for the social mind, we may well wonder on what evidence this claim rests. If the social mind exists we have no direct way of finding out what it thinks, and if we consider the tissue of mental forces operative in society, we shall find that it is a conglomeration of elements, exhibiting but little unity of purpose or clear perception of ends such as we find in the best or greatest individual minds. Consider what is called popular idealism – a medley of the vaguest spiritual exaltation with conceptions that have the most attenuated meaning – and contrast it with the clear-eyed vision and steadfast devotion of the great personalities of history. The result is not flattering to the social mind: and it may be safely said that if we ever get rid of the metaphysical illusion of a super-mind, the direct evidence for the alleged superiority of the popular mind will be seen to be negligible.

So far we have been dealing with theories according to which the social mind constitutes an actual collective consciousness.

McDougall rejects, at any rate provisionally, the theory of a collective consciousness in the sense of a unitary consciousness of society over and above that of the individuals comprised within it. Nevertheless there is in his view a group mind. By mind he understands an organized system of mental or purposive forces, and in this sense, he thinks, society may be said to possess a collective mind, for society is essentially an organization which can only be described or accounted for in terms of mind, i.e. it is constituted by the system of relations between the individual minds which are its units. The grounds for this assertion are threefold. In the first place, he argues that the individual minds that constitute society reciprocally imply and complement one another. The relations that subsist between them are intrinsic, they actually form part of the individual mind, so that society, i.e. the system of related minds, consists of the same stuff as individual minds, 'can only be described in terms of mind.' This, however, would not prove that society constitutes a mind. For clearly, though in order to give an account of society we must speak in terms of mind, it does not follow that the system that results from their inter-relation is itself a mind any more than a house that consists of bricks is itself a brick. Hence McDougall argues, in the second place, that at any one moment, the individual minds that enter society do not construct it, rather are they moulded and shaped by its subtle and multitudinous forces. Society is 'an organized system of forces, which has a life of its own, tendencies of its own, a power of moulding all its component individuals and a power of perpetuating itself as a self-identical system, subject only to slow and gradual change.'[1]

Thirdly, it is maintained, as it was by Durkheim, that the actions of society are or may be different from the 'mere sum' of the actions with which its several members would react to the situation in the absence of relations which render them a society. 'The thinking and acting of each man, in so far as he thinks and acts as a member of society, are very different from his thinking and acting as an isolated individual' (pp. 9, 10). With this is connected the argument, also urged by Durkheim, that society is 'greater' than the mere sum of its parts. McDougall goes so far as to argue that highly organized societies attain a degree of intelligence and morality above the level of its average members, even above that of its highest members (p. 53).

McDougall is anxious to mark off his view definitely from the view of German idealism, but it is hard to see in what the difference upon which he places such emphasis really consists. He quotes with approval the statement of Mr Barker that there is a social mind which is 'something that exists in and along with the separate minds of its members, and over and *above any sum of those minds created by mere addition*,' and he ascribes to the social mind of at any rate highly organized societies, a superiority in intelligence and morality to the average members and even the best. The only point of difference which is at all clearly brought out is that McDougall rejects the theory of a collective

[1] *The Group Mind*, p. 9.

consciousness with which he credits the Idealists. But it is extremely doubtful whether such a theory has ever been held by the latter. It is not to be found in Hegel, and Dr Bosanquet at any rate clearly repudiates it (*Mind*, Jan. 1921, p. 64). On the other hand, it should be mentioned that though Dr McDougall rejects the notion of a collective consciousness he constantly uses language which implies the existence of such a consciousness, as, e.g. when he alleges as against MacIver that the community acts, feels, wills and thinks (pp. 9, 10). The truth is that Mc-Dougall is working with two really different conceptions of the social mind. In the first place, we may mean by that term to indicate a society with a strongly developed *esprit de corps*, i.e. in McDougall's theory, a society in which every member has through long association come to have a definite idea of the group as a whole and to have formed a strong sentiment in relation to that whole by an extension of his self-regarding sentiment to include and embrace the interests of his group as a whole. But we may, in the second place, mean by the social mind, not that such an idea of the whole is necessarily present to the minds of all members, but rather that the group life rests on ideas, interests and values which form a coherent system and are not the product of any individual mind.

Now as to the former, we may, without accepting necessarily McDougall's account of the nature and development of altruism, agree that there may be some societies in which the members have a clear idea of the group as a whole and identify their good with the good of that whole. This may be true, for instance, of some families. But as an account of the national mind it seems to be palpably out of harmony with facts. If a nation exists only when in the mind of all its members there is present an idea of the nation as a whole and when they all identify their good with its good, then Britain is not a nation. The national mind, if the phrase be allowed at all for the mass of ideas operative in a society, is infinitely more complex and flexible than this theory would allow. If on the other hand, we elect to abide by the second and more concrete conception of the social mind, then Dr McDougall's view does not differ in essentials from the view of the Idealists which he condemns, and it is liable to the same objection as theirs, that, though it is true that society rests on ideas, purposes, traditions which are the result of a vast co-operation and are not produced by any individual mind, yet society does not possess the sort of unity which binds the parts of a personality together; that the theory confuses unity of content with unity of process, and above all that it carries with it all the dangerous consequences, as is exemplified by McDougall and the Idealists alike, enumerated in the beginning of this chapter.

The argument based on the alleged superiority of the social mind to the 'sum of its parts' also is ambiguous. We may mean in the first place, that a highly organized group arrives at decisions intellectually and morally superior to the decisions which any of its members, even the best, could arrive at in isolation. This is frequently dogmatically asserted, but it may well be doubted whether it is always or even frequently the case. In complex societies in particular, it may well be urged that public decisions do not as a rule exceed in nobility or clearness of vision the opinions of its greatest members. But in so far as this superiority is exhibited, it is simply due to co-operation and to the fact that where the machinery for collective deliberation is good, members of a society are likely to learn from one another and each to reveal such aspects of the matter under discussion as may not have been noted by the others. One fails to see what need there is in this reference for a social mind in any other sense than that of several individuals' minds working in co-operation. But we may, in the second place, mean by this superiority the fact that social traditions, intellectual and moral institutions, and the like, are not the product of any one mind and exceed in magnitude and weight the contents of any individual mind. But surely traditions and institutions are in themselves nothing; they have to be sustained and re-interpreted by individuals from generation to generation, and though they exceed in content the contents of any individual mind, they are not greater than all individual minds in co-operation.

McDougall frequently argues that society has a mental life

which is not the mere sum of the mental lives of its units existing as independent units, and that we could not deduce the nature of the whole from the nature of its units; but this argument seems to me purely verbal. We never can get at individual units absolutely apart from all social relations. Further, McDougall himself agrees with MacIver that these social relations are intrinsic to the individual and exist only within him; but if we consider individuals as we find them, as members of groups, as possessing relationship to others, what is there in society over and above individual minds formed into groups? The idea that we can get a 'mere sum' of isolated individuals and contrast them with the concrete social entity is a gratuitous assumption to which, it seems to me, no meaning can be attached.

Nor does McDougall succeed in countering the argument against the existence of social minds based on the complexity and intersection of groups in modern societies. 'Social organizations,' MacIver urges, 'occur of every kind and every degree of universality. If England has a collective mind, why not Birmingham and why not each of its wards? If a nation has a collective mind, so have a church and a trade union. And we shall have collective minds that are parts of greater collective minds and collective minds that intersect other collective minds.' To which Dr McDougall replies: 'By this my withers are quite unwrung. What degree of organization is necessary before a society can properly be said to enjoy collective mental life or have a group mind is a question of degree, and the exponent of the group mind is under no obligation to return a precise answer to this question' (p. 11). But it seems to me that the intersection and overlapping of social groups due to the fact that the same individuals may be members of various groups at the same time points to the important fact that these groupings represent only partial phases or aspects of the lives of individuals and do not therefore possess the *same kind* of unity and concreteness as that possessed by individual minds, and to the equally important fact that the individual is much more than can be expressed in terms of his membership in social groupings, and that he possesses a kind of unity, a core of being which is not exhausted in those memberships. In some respects the analysis of the group mind given by McDougall is more valuable than that of Durkheim and, as far as I know, than that of most other writers. It does, namely, take into consideration the difference in mentality of different kinds of social aggregates and points out the way in which we may conceive of a progressive development of mind and of the elements of conscious control in society. Fundamentally, however, he appears to waver between two different conceptions of the social mind; and though he repudiates the conception of a collective consciousness he does use phraseology which implies a belief in such consciousness. This perhaps has led him to ascribe to the social mind superiority over the individual mind, as in his discussion of public opinion, and to a dangerous contrast between the good of the whole as contrasted with the good of its component members.[1] It may also to some extent account for his essentially aristocratic and conservative attitude, for the social mind cannot speak for itself and is best interpreted apparently by the 'best' elements of the community.

So far our account has not yielded any coherent view of the nature of the social mind. But, of course, the theories of the social mind were elaborated to meet a real problem, the problem of the kind of reality that belongs to social wholes. They clearly are unities of mind, since they consist of minds in interrelation and the relations themselves are dependent on mental factors. Nevertheless it seems mistaken to regard community as a mind, just as it is mistaken to regard communal wholes as organisms, though the relations between their constituent parts are organic. 'Social inquiry,' as Professor Hobhouse says, 'suffers from nothing so much as a lack of technical terms or of suitable metaphor to supply the place of technical terms. It has to use words derived from other orders of experience and conceptions elaborated in other sciences. What we must most eschew is any term suggesting a form of unity realized in some other whole than the particular social whole which we are considering.'[2] An important source of confusion is certainly the neglect to dis-

---

[1] cf. *The Group Mind*, p. 172.
[2] *The Metaphysical Theory of the State*, p. 131.

tinguish the different degrees of unity attained by different kinds of social aggregates.[1] In a crowd, for instance, there is a sort of unity due to the presence of a common object of attention and to the fact that the object has attractive power for the majority of the members, based on their previous experience, inherited or natural characteristics, and the like. But this unity is relatively simple and does not exhibit the delicate and subtle interplay and adaptation of part to part which we find in developed organisms. It is a unity achieved by suggestion, i.e. by an appeal to a dominant emotional tendency and an inhibition of conflicting tendencies. It is not that there is a fusion of personalities or an operation of some mysterious collective consciousness, but rather that each individual becomes under the circumstances less critical, less responsible, more confident, credulous, more suggestible. No doubt each individual in a crowd feels, thinks and acts differently from what he would do were he in isolation. But the difference is merely a case of response to a different environment, and certainly does not need for its explanation the appeal to a mysterious common mind, somehow created by aggregation.

In more organized groupings additional factors come into play. The unity and cohesion of associations depends on the degree of clearness with which the purpose of the particular associations is grasped by its members and the strength of the sentiments which they have each developed for it and the emotional warmth with which they identify their interests with its interests. In the case of the majority of associations a clear grasp of ends and a high degree of emotional attachment are only found in a few members, while the rest are kept in the association largely by habit and suggestion, perhaps by a dimly felt need for it. Common purposes and common sentiments, however, do not need for their explanation a common mind. They are ideas entertained and sentiments felt by individuals with reference to similar or identical objects. Only a confusion of process and content necessitates the appeal to the common

---

[1] Dr McDougall, of course, emphasizes the difference between the crowd and organized society.

mind. In any case the organic character of associations is much exaggerated and they certainly do not possess the substantive continuity which characterizes individual minds. The kind of reality that belongs to the community, of which associations are merely parts, and which includes, in addition to them, all the relations of harmony and conflict, of competition and co-operation between individuals which escape organization, is the most complex and difficult to define. To say that it is a mind is not in any sense illuminating. It is made up of a thousand manifold interactions, of a maze of interests, conflicting and comple-mentary, of unity within unity in bewildering variety. The rela-tion that subsists between one individual and others in a crowd differ from those that bind him to the associations to which he belongs. These in turn differ from one association to another, according to the closeness of the ties that bind him to them, and from the relations that bind him to the all-embracing com-munity. It must therefore be admitted that the problem of the relation of the individual to the social wholes to which he belongs is more complex than the theory of the social mind allows for. A more positive account of these relations will be attempted later. Meanwhile we may note that in the notion of the common mind are really included the following elements:

1. Mental elements common to members of a given society, modes of reaction due to hereditary structure, racial charac-teristics and the like.

2. Common traditions, moral and intellectual, (*a*) embodied in books, in institutions, laws, customs, etc.; (*b*) not crystallized but 'floating' about or partially expressed in public opinion, tendencies in art and literature, popular movements.

3. Social sentiments, i.e. sentiments of loyalty, existing of course in individual minds, which have for their nucleus, or cluster around, social groupings of various kinds. The latter in particular make plausible the theory of a social mind, for we can feel loyalty to a group in a manner analogous to the loyalty we feel to an individual person. It should, however, be remembered that those who do not accept the theory of the social mind, do not deny the reality of social groupings. They are as real as the

individuals of which they are composed, and for certain purposes, e.g. legal and moral obligation, they may be looked upon
as persons, but that does not mean that they really are persons or
minds. As to the common elements indicated in the second and
first groups above, an account will be given of them which does
not imply a social mind, and it will be shown that no unity of
mind corresponds to those common elements. Before dealing
with these questions, however, it will be well to discuss a doctrine very closely connected with the wider theory of the social
mind, the doctrine, namely, of the general will. To this we turn
in the next chapter.

The Conception of a General Will

THE CONCEPTION of a general will has played an important role in political philosophy since the days of Rousseau. It has, in the main, been used as a basis for what may be termed a monistic theory of sovereignty and law, but it is noteworthy that many of those who are now insisting on the claims of minor associations within the State do so on the ground that these minor associations possess a 'real' or general will of their own.[1] The literature on the subject, and on the kindred problem of the personality of associations, is enormous, but there are not many attempts at a really systematic analysis. The object of this chapter is to deal critically with some of these problems, and in particular with the doctrine of a real will, as worked out by Professor Bosanquet. The attempts referred to fall into five groups, which are more or less clearly marked off, though they are not mutually exclusive, and for convenience of discussion they will be dealt with separately.

In the first place, the general will is conceived as coming to be when every individual in a group or society, or a compact majority of such a group or society, has a conception or idea of the group as a whole and identifies his good with the good of that whole. This would appear to be the view of Dr McDougall. Sometimes, as is the case with Novicov, the presence of such an idea of the whole is required only in the case of the social *élite*, i.e., the actual leaders (not necessarily the government) of thought and action in a community. In Novicov's view ('Con-

---

[1] cf. Gierke, *Genossenschaftsrecht*, vol. 3, and *Das Wesen der menschlichen Verbände*; Maitland's Introduction to Gierke's *Medieval Political Theories*; Figgis, *Churches in the Modern State*; and much of the literature of Guild Socialism.

science et Volonté Générale') Society is a psychical organism, and the social *élite* constitutes for him a common sensorium, analogous to the brain of an individual organism.

In the second place, a will is said to be general when a decision is arrived at by deliberate discussion, aiming at a real integration of differences, i.e. at utilizing the contribution of each constituent member of a group, and not at mere blending of individual wishes. This apparently is the view of Professor Mackenzie, according to whom the idea of a general will involves: (1) the concurrence of a number of people in a single decision; (2) the fact that the decision is taken with reference to the good of the whole group, and not merely by a balancing of individual wishes. The first of these conditions, however, is watered down to a mere vague desire or feeling, on the part of those by whom the decision is made, that it shall be in harmony with the point of view of others whom it affects. When this qualification is made, it is clear that the decision is really arrived at, in most cases, by a comparatively few individuals, although they may take into account the opinions and desires of the majority of the people for whom they are acting, in so far as these can be ascertained. In this sense the term is innocuous, but not particularly important. It is merely a rather confusing way of saying, e.g. that governmental acts should be based on some form of consent, active or passive, on the part of the majority of the governed; and it has the defect that it hides the fact that in actual groups, especially States, action taken is often the result not of unanimous co-operative agreement, on the part of a majority, but only of a comparatively small number of people. In the hands of some writers, e.g. Miss Follett, the integration of differences, spoken of above, may be connected with the doctrine of the 'confluence' of minds or the compounding of states of consciousness, and in that case the general will is conceived as constituting an actual entity, the product or result of the interpenetration of individual minds, in what is called the social process.

In the third place, it comes to be recognized that society as a whole and the social good can only be common contents of consciousness in the very highest stages of social development.[1] It is, however, claimed that in all societies possessing a certain amount of continuity and independence there must be other common contents of thought and will, with the result that its members, when confronted with the same situation, or stimulated by the same objects, will experience the same inner reaction. There may be moments or periods in the life of a nation, it is admitted, when there is little community of thought, feeling and will and then social self-consciousness is at a minimum. But this is the case, also, in individuals, except that for them the moments of conscious activity are more frequent and last relatively longer. According to this view, the individual self is regarded as a combination of certain temporary and transient contents of consciousness, with those which are more constant, such as certain enduring relations of the inner life, and certain experiences relating to the body. Through this combination or union the constant is set over against and contrasted with the variable, and becomes, as such, relatively clear and explicit, thus resulting in self-consciousness. So, too, in society there are certain contents of consciousness which are more or less permanent and constant, e.g. the traditions and the consciousness of a common past, which are at the background of the common mind, and when over against these there appears a new experience, perhaps threatening them, society becomes self-conscious and is capable of self-conscious volition. Compare the Greeks against the Persians, the Germans against Napoleon, and the like.

In dealing with these views we must note, at the outset, two important distinctions. In the first place, we must distinguish the act of volition from the object willed. In the second place, we must distinguish definite acts of will from dispositions or habits of will, i.e. capacities to will when confronted with a certain situation. We may say that as a result of group-life, definite acts of will, or the more or less permanent systems of dispositions or habits of will of the individuals composing it, may be influenced and determined by an idea of the interest not only of the individual, but of the whole group. Where this is the

---

[1] cf. Barth, *Geschichte der Philosophie als Soziologie*.

case, in regard to every individual member of a group or a compact majority, we can speak of the will of such members as general, meaning by that not that they all aim at a universal object (which has not been shown), nor that there is *a* general will, as distinct from a number of wills, but merely that there is sufficient community of ideas and ideals to influence the specific acts of will of the individuals concerned, to induce them to take common action, or to arrive at joint decisions. We are not in such cases entitled to speak of a *will of the whole*, but merely of a *will of all*, determined by a sense of the *good of the whole*. The acts of volition must remain individual, concrete. The will of the people can only be a joint will, due to a concurrence of such acts, though the latter may resemble one another, because of the similarity of their contents, or because they are all influenced by an idea of the good of the whole, or rather by what is conceived to be the good of the whole.

Whether such a general will exists or not is a question of fact, to be determined with regard to each grouping by special investigation. Generally the psychological forces that ultimately issue in a public act would seem to contain little that can be called will in the strict sense of the word. They are rather an impalpable congeries of elements including blind impulses, dimly foreseen ends, unconscious or half-conscious inferences, habits and prejudices. Even great political decisions are rarely arrived at as a result of clear co-operative thinking, on the part of all members of a group or even of a majority.[1] If, with Dr McDougall, we confine the collective will to those cases of group actions which are the result of a determination of the will of each member of the group, by a sentiment of regard for the group as a whole, and by an idea of the good of that whole, the sphere of collective volition is exceedingly narrow. It may exist, e.g. in some families, or in some small groups working for specific objects; but in the large groupings of the modern world, the existence of such a will is a hope and aspiration, rather than a fact. The State in particular includes complex groupings with many divergent interests. Such groupings, moreover, develop a

---

[1] cf. Graham Wallas, *Human Nature in Politics*, ch. 3.

collective selfishness, often in conflict with the good of the whole. There may be, there no doubt is, present in the majority of the people a diffused sense of interest in the whole, a vague desire to contribute actively or passively to the maintenance of the social structure, but this can hardly be called a will. The reasons that determine the adoption of any one idea or plan of action, and the rejection of others, are often found in anything but a conscious recognition of their inherent truth or value; and in so far as there is such conscious thought, it is confined to a few persons who, in many cases, are high-minded and disinterested, but in others deliberately foster the spread of certain ideas, in the interests of certain classes, rather than of the people as a whole. Though, in some cases unconsciously, the process of selection is often biased. In the case of complex groupings, we may say, therefore, that in so far as there is present self-conscious volition, it is not general, and in so far as the psychical forces operating in a society are general, they are not will. Similar remarks apply to Dr Barth's treatment. The kind of self-consciousness of which he speaks can exist only at periods of great crises in the life of a nation, when the whole of society is in danger. It is only in such cases, when a nation feels that all its permanent possessions are threatened, that it will act as a whole. Even then it seems doubtful whether we get an example of really self-conscious volition. For it is during such periods that very often the lower impulses and instincts of a mob get free play. It might, perhaps, be urged that in the case of individual volition, too, the existence of self-conscious volition has its basis in a precipitate of habits, instincts, and dispositions, but while in the case of the individual, the instinctive elements are fused with and overlaid by conscious ideas in the same personality, in the case of society, consciousness of society as a whole may be present in the minds of its most enlightened and public-spirited members, yet the majority of the people may remain at the level of habit or instinct, so far as their relation to the whole is concerned. Here again, therefore, in so far as there is will, it is not general, and so far as the forces operating are general, they are not will.

We can now discuss a fourth view of the general will, some-what analogous to Dr Barth's, but more thoroughly worked out – that, namely, of Wundt,[1] This view is based on an analysis of the mutual implications of presentation and will. Will cannot be bare activity, but implies presentation, as content and motive. On the other hand, presentation implies a presentative activity. Presentations, in fact, owe their origin, according to Wundt, to the action of one will on another. It follows that any concrete will pre-supposes other wills. This leads Wundt to the concep-tion of reality as a series of will-unities – *eine Stufenfolge von Willenseinheiten* – which through mutual determination, or reciprocal action, i.e. presentative activity, develop into a series of will-complexes of various extent. The unity which attaches to any concrete empirical will is only relative. The individual is really a general will, uniting within itself will-forms of lower grade, for bare individual activity is a limiting point, which is never actually met with in experience. Again, at the other extreme, we may conceive a general will of all human-ity, uniting all its members and groups of members for common purposes, and finally the religious consciousness postulates the will of God, which is the highest and last unity, at once the source of the common spiritual possessions of mankind, and the conditions of their realization. The general will (*Gesamtwille*), according to this view, is very complex, and includes within itself many forms of unity, varying in extent and power. But the reality which belongs to it, and, within it, to the wider and narrower forms of it, is not hypothetical but actual. The true reality of the individual self is not to be found in some under-lying substance or substratum, but in actual spiritual life, in conscious activity – *Bewusstseinstätigkeit* – in the extent of its capacity to concentrate within itself, and give expression to the common spiritual possession of mankind, the will-directions or tendencies of the age. Once we abandon the view of the soul or self as a separately and independently existing substance or sub-stratum, we are justified, Wundt thinks, in assigning to the general will a degree of reality not less than that of the

[1] cf. *System der Philosophie* and *Ethik*.

individual will. The movements of civilization, the growth of cultures, are indications of a really common life which cannot be a merely fortuitous resultant of individual aims, related externally to one another. We must, however, Wundt warns us, beware of attaching too much importance to the general or objective will at the cost of individual wills. This is just as one-sided as the narrow individualism of the opposed theories of psychological and ethical atomism. There are individuals who have so mastered the ideas or feelings which move their community, and who are so gifted to give these effective expression, that they have come to be not merely the agents and creators of the aims of the general will, but are able to impose and impress features of their own upon the general will, and stamp with their own character the tendency of the time. This, however, is not incompatible with the reality of the general will, since the latter is essentially very complex and is really a series of will-unities.

Wundt's treatment has the merit that it does not involve the conception of the general will as an entity independent of individual minds, and that it allows room for the existence of smaller units within the general will. At the same time, it is liable to dangerous misinterpretations, and fundamentally it suffers from the fatal ambiguity that attaches to the word presentation. This, of course, is not the place for examining the validity of the assertion that presentations are themselves will-activities. It will, at any rate, be conceded that, if they are of the nature of will or activity, the activity spoken of is not *the activity* in and through which they are apprehended. If this distinction be admitted, then the reasons for regarding higher complexes as having the same reality as the individual will fall to the ground. For the acts in and through which presentations are apprehended must always be individual specific acts, belonging to different individuals, though, of course, several individuals may unite, act as one body, have presentations in common, i.e. be aware of the same objects and aim at the same ideals.

The distinction referred to is often ignored by Wundt himself. He speaks, for example, of presentative activity as being the same thing as presentation, and if this view is joined with his view that the reality of the self consists in activity, the door is open for the 'mind stuff' theory and the theory of the group-consciousness, such as we find, e.g. in Durkheim. By the latter, presentations are regarded as 'partially autonomous' realities which have the power of mutual attraction and repulsion and of forming ever new syntheses. Thus there come to be, according to the latter, social or collective presentations which belong to the social mind, and are spoken of as 'exterior' to the individual mind; and although Durkheim often makes it clear that the social presentations can exist only in individual minds, yet he also speaks of the social mind as an actual entity, over and above individual minds – a new creation *sui generis*. Thus he speaks of the collective consciousness as the highest form of the psychic life and as a *consciousness of consciousnesses*.[1] Now there is a sense in which contents of presentations have an independent being. Mythologies, e.g. have a way of growing by a sort of inherent power of ideas to combine and re-combine. But this really means that an idea once having been thought out by an individual and communicated to others must necessarily modify the ideas of those others. There is no warrant, however, for speaking of collective presentations as constituting a mind, or soul, or consciousness.

We can now deal with the doctrine of the general will as it is worked out by Professor Bosanquet, and in a modified form by other Idealists. In essence, this doctrine consists of the following three elements: In the first place, it is maintained, that both the particular acts of the will of an individual, and the system of volitional dispositions which we may call his character or his 'standing will', imply a real will or a will of the true self. By this is not meant the actual character of a man, the permanent underlying nature or bent of an individual, but rather a supposed rational or good self, an ideal will based on 'a fully articulated idea of the best life for man.' In the second place, it is argued that the latter is essentially social in character, is, in fact, qualitatively identical in all individuals, and therefore constitutes one will. And, in the third place, that this one will, described as 'real' or 'general', is embodied in the State.

[1] cf. *Les formes élementaires de la vie religieuse*, p. 23.

I propose to confine attention here to the first two of these propositions.

(*a*) In the first place, then, the real will is contrasted with the actual will, or the will of the individual in the ordinary routine of life. The latter consists of acts which are incomplete, imperfect, 'abstract and fragmentary', and they point beyond themselves to a system which would give them meaning – a system of connected volitions or dispositions, which is held or bound together by organizing principles. Of such principles we may be conscious, but even where they are not consciously appreciated by the individual they are none the less, it is maintained, implied in his conduct. This so far may be granted, but from such arguments it would not follow that the real will is rational or good. Surely it will not be denied that the standing or permanent wills of most individuals are far from haromonious unities governed by rational principles. It would seem, then, that by the real will is not meant merely the standing or permanent will which actually belongs to individuals, but an ideal will – in other words, the will as it ought to be. Such an ideal will is, however, it is argued, implied in the actual will. For no object of action is ever completely satisfactory, ever exhausts all that our full nature demands. At any given moment we do not know what we *really* want, what would completely satisfy our whole personality. To discover what we really want, we should have to correct our desires of the moment by a comparison with what we desire at other moments, and with what other people desire; we should have, in short, to institute a process of criticism and examination into the conditions of a good and harmonious life; and when this process had been gone through, our own will would come back to us in a shape which we should almost fail to recognize. This reconstructed will is, it is maintained, our real will. It is, therefore, the rational or good will, the will as it ought to be, the will as determined by an idea of perfection; and, though it transcends by far that at which we consciously aim, it is nevertheless implied in the latter, since it alone can give significance to the practical life.

The value of the argument seems to me to depend on two

things: (1) upon the question in what sense a person may be said to will 'what is implied' in his actual volitions, and (2) upon the meaning of the word 'real' in this connexion. Firstly, then, if by the term will is meant actually conscious choice, it might be denied that a person wills anything except an object of which he is distinctly aware. This restriction of the term will, however, may be inconvenient. Recent psychology has familiarized us with the fact that often our conscious motives are only a 'camouflage' for deeper wants of which we may be unconscious, and it would be, in some cases, carping at words to say that these deeper wants do not represent our real will. Granting this, however, there is no reason for supposing that in any particular case, the discovery of such deeper motives and their complete enumeration would reveal a rational or good will. On the contrary, it may well bring to light deep and far-reaching conflict. Again, by what is implied may be meant all those courses of conduct, plans and aims which a man might admit were involved in any particular volitional act of his, if he reflected critically on that act. Here, too, in any particular case, there is no reason to suppose that such a scheme of life must necessarily be good or rational, though no doubt it would *appear* so to the individual concerned. It would seem, then, that for the purpose of the above argument the phrase 'what is implied' must mean all those courses of action which a perfectly rational person would see were involved in any act or system of acts of an individual. In what sense, now, can this be said to be the real will not of completely rational persons, but of ordinary mortals? I think that what is in the mind of the thinkers who hold this view is that the sense of moral and political obligation cannot be explained unless we assume the presence in each individual of an idea, however vague and ill-defined, of a best and ultimate good. This is sometimes stated in a way which would seem to imply that when I say I ought to do this, I mean that I will to do this. Thus Professor Bosanquet says:—'The imperative claim of the will that wills itself is our own inmost nature and we cannot throw it off. This is the root of political obligation.' As against this, it must be said that though it might well be argued that what is ethically obligatory must be psychologically capable of being willed, ethical obligation does not consist in being willed any more than an object known consists in its being known. The fact that I will, or that my real self or anyone else wills a thing, is not an adequate reason why it should or ought to be done, unless there is a reason to show that it is good that it should be done. The moral order, in other words, is something objective, and obligation consists in the claim which such a moral order has upon us, but neither the moral order nor the obligation consists in, or is identical with, acts of will, human or divine.

Apart from the misconception referred to, we may admit that the sense of moral obligation and moral conduct do imply some sense of a possible perfection, some dim awareness of an ultimate good struggling to assert itself in the individual or in a society of individuals. But can this be rightly described as a real will in contrast with which the actual will is regarded as illusory or fragmentary? It is surely one thing to say that a conception of a possible good is implied in our will and quite another that such a good is really willed. The idea of an ultimate good, after all, is only a vague schema or assumption resembling the assumption of the principle of the uniformity of nature that is held to be implied in scientific investigation; and from this schema as such, nothing can be deduced as regards the details of conduct. By calling it real, however, more definiteness is ascribed to it than really belongs to it, and this has disastrous consequences when further it is identified with the general will as embodied in law, for the ground is then prepared for the argument that what is imposed on the individual by the general will is really imposed upon him by himself and in this way any amount of interference with him can be theoretically justified.

In the second place, the use of the word 'real' in this connexion implies the idealist doctrine of 'degrees of reality', which, of course, cannot here be examined. I should say that a thing is either real or not real, and that, therefore, the actual will is just as real as the 'real' will, if by the latter we mean the permanent or standing will, though the former is relatively to it transitory.

If, on the other hand, as seems to be the case, by the real will is meant a completely rational will with a definitely articulate organic system of purposes, then such a will is not real at all, but ideal.

(b) *The General Will.* – The real will then, is the rational or good will, the will as it ought to be. Now such a will, it is argued, is in quality and content identical in all individuals. It is not merely a joint will or will of all, but is rather of the nature of a thread of connexion permeating all individual wills, or a universal in Bosanquet's sense of the term, i.e. a scheme which realizes itself in particular wills, but is more permanent and greater than any actual will. The content of all rational wills, in other words, is a 'concrete universal', an organic system of those ends and purposes which would completely satisfy the demands of human nature. From such identity of content, an identity of substantive unity and continuity of existence is inferred and the general will is then spoken of as a person, a *moi commun*, a will, an experience of which individuals are imperfect manifestations. Society thus comes to be conceived as a single experience, a continuous self-identical being of psychical contents. Particular individuals, in and through whom this 'social universal' realizes itself, are organizations or connexions of content, more or less articulate, within this system. All have within them the active spirit or form of the whole, and as a result, they strive after unity and individuality, i.e. completely articulate experience. To the extent to which they succeed, they become more and more articulate, and in the end, they would merge or become identical with the single articulate experience which is the whole. Separateness, therefore, is not an ultimate character of the individual, for in substance and content the minds and wills of individuals are universal, 'communicable, expansive'.

The argument rests on the assumption that identity of content involves identity of existence. Waiving the question how far all rational wills of finite individuals must be identical in content (though it does not seem to me that this has been proved), we may note that Bosanquet himself has drawn attention to the distinction between ideas as psychical existents and ideas as

contents; and, at first sight, it might appear that once this distinction is made the argument for the unity of minds in society,
based on their community of experience, breaks down. For
though ideas as contents may be common, ideas as psychical
existents never can be. When two people are aware of the same
objects, the acts of awareness considered as psychical occurrences cannot be the same, though they might be regarded as
resembling one another. Professor Bosanquet himself seems
sometimes to admit this. Thus he says: 'No one would attempt
to overthrow what we have called the formal distinctness of selves
or souls. This consists in the impossibility that one finite centre
of experience should possess as its own immediate experience,
the immediate experience of another.'[1] Yet it would seem that
this formal distinctness is compatible with a fundamental same-
ness or identity. How is this to be explained? It seems to me
that the root of the matter lies in the fact that Professor Bosanquet is not really serious with the distinction between psychical
existence or immediacy, as he calls it, and content, and that he
tends virtually to deny the reality of the former. Immediacy or
psychical existence is taken to be not a part of the series of
mental acts or occurrences which we call the mind. 'It is a
phase and not a stratum of experience.'[2] By this is presumably
meant that it is a phase into which contents may enter, and out of
which they may pass. Acts of apprehension are, as they are also
described by him, forms which contents may assume. 'Any content of apprehension or comprehension may become a state of
our mind.' 'All our objective apprehension is something which
is capable of taking the shape of a mental state, i.e. of becoming
immediate.'[3] The content is taken to be a continuum, having an
independent reality prior to the acts of apprehension, which
latter are merely a limitation of it, a partition introduced into it,
due presumably to the fact that they are dependent on different
bodies. Thus we are told that different persons are 'organizations of content which a difference of quality generally, though

[1] *The Value and Destiny of the Individual*, p. 47.
[2] *Logic*, vol. 2, p. 301.
[3] Ibid. p. 300.

not strictly dependent on or belonging to different bodies, prevents from being wholly blended'. In respect of content, however, it is maintained they are identical and confluent.

It seems clear, from what has been said, that the whole argument in favour of the confluence of minds, or their inclusion in a larger mind, is based upon a hypostatization of contents and a denial of the reality of acts of experience. As against this whole position it must be urged:

(1) Contents never *become* states of mind. They are either constituents of a state of mind aware of itself, or references to objects or truths other than the acts by which they are apprehended.

(2) The contents cannot be regarded as having an independent existence prior to the acts of apprehension or comprehension. They are inherent in acts of consciousness or awareness resulting from the direction of the latter upon themselves or upon objects other than themselves. In neither case can independent existence be properly ascribed to them.

(3) It follows that acts of consciousness, say of two persons or of the same individual at different times, directed on the same object, will resemble one another, and, if we like to sum up all such acts and include them under the term experience, we can say that experience is a universal in the sense that it is a class of objects (i.e. acts), resembling one another or possessing identity of character. But two acts whose contents were exactly the same would still be two acts and similarly two minds.

(4) The question, however, might still be pressed: Does not unity or identity of content, in the case of thought or will, so penetrate the existence of the separate acts of will or thought as to convert unity of content into unity of existence? It seems to me that the thinkers who argue in this manner do so because they really regard contents or essences as themselves existents, and, in particular, if the problem is approached from the side of ideals and purposes, because of the belief they entertain that the ideals and purposes of human subjects are in a sense *already realized* in a Universal Mind. Thus Professor Bosanquet quotes with approval Green's statement that 'when that which is being

developed is itself a selfconscious subject, the end of its becoming must really exist, not merely for, but in or as a self-conscious subject. There must be eternally such a subject, which is all that the self-conscious subject, as developed in time, has the possibility of becoming, in which the ideal of the human spirit or all that it has in it to become, is completely realized'. Similarly, Professor Muirhead argues that though actions belong to individuals, yet 'their purposes, so far as they are harmonized, are included in the organic system of purposes which we have agreed can only be real in so far as they are the purposes of a Universal Mind'; and he makes it clear that in the supreme mind the meanings and purposes of finite minds must, *in some sense, be fulfilled*.[1] Now all this seems to me to involve a hypostatization of ideals and the denial of the distinction between truth and existence. Ideals are contents of thought and will, and I fail to see that the non-existential character which attaches to them is altered when the mind that entertains them or thinks them is the mind of God. I fail to see, also, what is gained for the religious or social life, by insisting on a unity of existence as between minds. Is it not enough if they can be shown to have common purposes and be striving after the same ideals? Professor Bosanquet argues that the standing will of each individual, the system of his connected volitions, implies and is implied in other similar systems of other individuals; and hence he concludes that there is a single inclusive system of which all particular wills are limitations or parts.[2] Leaving aside the argument that such a complete system of wills is an ideal rather than a fact, it seems to me clear that the kind of unity that such a system would exhibit throws no light whatever on the problem of the confluence of wills. Granting that any will, having for its object a part of such a complete system, wills 'by implication' the rest of the system, all that follows would be that all the particular wills would will the same object, but it would not follow at all that any particular will is existentially identical with any other will or with the will of society. The fact that the realization of my purposes is depen-

[1] *Problems of Science and Philosophy*, p. 133.
[2] *Mind*, January, 1920, p. 80.

dent on the existence of other human beings and the realization of their purposes on mine does not involve that they must be I, or I they; and the continuum of mental acts, which constitutes the phases of a self, does not lose its existential unity because their contents are identical in character with the contents of the mental acts of another self.

In yet another way, Professor Bosanquet tries to show that society and individual minds are really the same fabric or structure regarded from different points of view. The mind, it is argued, is made up of apperceptive masses or systems of ideas, each with its controlling or dominant idea. Social institutions or social groupings also consist of systems of ideas, held together by a dominant purpose which connects them in such a way as to render possible the fulfilment of the function of the whole. A social institution is the meeting point of many minds, is, in other words, 'a system of appercipient systems by which the minds that take part in them are kept in correspondence'. Further, social groupings each with its dominant purpose, may aid or support, one another, or again, they may be divergent or conflicting, but at bottom, they must be organs of a single pervading life, and cannot be ultimately irreconcilable. From this point of view, society is seen to be of the nature of a continuous or self-identical being consisting of activities which by their differences are made to play into one another and to form a thoroughly welded whole or 'world'. Now, it is of course true, that society and individuals are made up of the same elements since society consists of individuals. But, in the first place, unless we believe in the compounding of states of consciousness or else deny the distinction between act and content, the argument does not prove that the social mind constitutes a unity of existence in the same sense in which the series of states of consciousness which we call a mind, constitutes a unity of existence; and, in the second place, the problem we have to face is, whether social acts, or deliverances of the social mind, the purposes embodied in social institutions, *exhaust* the character of the individual. Professor Bosanquet seems to start not with individuals and their purposes, but with the universal 'human nature' as a kind of organic scheme of functions or purposes; and, theoretically, individual existence or 'uniqueness of form' should be accompanied by uniqueness of matter or content; every finite individual ought to have one special function to perform in society – a function which would never be performed by any other individual. Such an individual would be 'a true particular of the social universal'. Were this the case, there would, in Professor Bosanquet's view, still be no ground for ascribing exclusiveness to selves, for individual minds would then have to be regarded as organic parts of a single whole, and these organic parts would *be* the whole, would be, i.e. ways in which the Universal manifests itself, or assumes special modification. This latter argument clearly rests on Professor Bosanquet's doctrine of the 'concrete universal', and it is open to anyone who does not accept that doctrine to maintain that the parts never are identical with one another or with the system that includes them. In point of fact, however, the theoretical 'one mind, one function', is never realized in society. The capacities of individuals are 'arbitrary and contingent'. One mind may repeat, overlap, and comprehend the experiences of other minds. The contents of a mind may vary 'from what just suffices for a function like that of an ant to a self which possesses the frame-work and very much of the detail of an entire society'. Yet does not the fact of repetition and overlapping prove that the universal 'human nature' is wrongly conceived as an individual, does it not prove that particularity is more than an appearance and refuses to be swallowed up in the whole? Is there not here a confusion between the universal 'human nature' or 'human capacity or potentiality' which does not consist at all of particular existents, and society, which does consist of a number of particulars related to one another in various ways, and which, though it possesses a kind of unity of its own, cannot possibly have the kind of unity that belongs to a concept? What is meant by the 'true particular of the social universal' depends on the meaning of the latter phrase. If the reference is to society, then any actual individual is a member of it. If, however, the reference is to an organic scheme of purposes or to human capacity, then the true particular is not an individual at all. Further, the 'true particular', in the former sense, is never exhausted in the social relations in which he enters. He possesses a kind of self-determination, a substantive unity and continuity, which is never merged in these relations. He is the centre of a rich diversity of relations which are but imperfectly expressed in social institutions, and so far from saying that the individual is an expression or reflection of society from 'a unique point of view or special angle', we should say that society is an expression or reflection of individuals from a unique point of view or special angle. The appercipient systems which constitute the common material of individuals and society contain in the case of each individual elements of feeling, emotion and bodily sensation which are exclusively theirs and incommunicable. It must, I think, be apparent that the real weight of the argument in favour of a general will rests, not on a psychological analysis of *de facto* states of mind, or even of human purposes as conceived by the generality of actual individuals, but upon an inferred real will in which all human purposes are unified and harmonized. Now, Professor Bosanquet himself argues that a general will of Humanity as a whole, Humanity as an ethical ideal, is a 'type or a problem rather than a fact'. So long as we confine ourselves to facts, may not the same be said of the general will of any existing state? If, on the other hand, the real will is the ideal will; if, especially, we have in mind a rational system of purposes in some sense already fulfilled in the Universal Mind, does not then a greater reality attach to the general will of Humanity, in which the wills of existing states would be harmonized and unified, than to the general wills of the several states which, in relation to Humanity, can only be regarded as particular?[1]

Summing up this discussion, we may say:

1. There may be something in each individual, and, therefore, in a society of individuals, which responds to a conception of an ultimate good or idea of perfection. This, however, is badly described as a 'real' will. The actual wills of individuals contain

[1] cf. Rousseau, *A Discourse on Political Economy.*

many elements which are not in correspondence with such an
ideal of perfection, and these elements are quite as 'real' as the
'real' will. If, on the other hand, by the latter is meant a fully
articulate scheme of organized purposes or ends, this is, strictly
speaking, an ideal and not a real will.

2. The crux of the problem, however, really lies in the identification of this ideal will with the general will. This seems to rest
on a confusion between content and existence; and breaks down
utterly if we insist on keeping that distinction clearly before our
minds. Even if all wills be shown to aim at a universal or general
object, they would still as psychical existents remain distinct.

3. Since there is no such thing as a general will, the question
whether it is embodied in the State does not arise. This does not
mean that the State and other forms of community do not
exhibit a kind of unity, but only that the unity which they possess is a relation between the individuals constituting them,
based on community of purposes and ideals, and that such a
unity need not be hypostatized and spoken of as a person or
will.[1] For the purposes of social theory, what is required is not a
common self but a common good. It is not at all necessary to
prove that individual minds have a unity and identity of existence, but merely that they have a oneness of spiritual content in
the sense that they must strive for the same common good and
be animated by the same ideals. When we speak of society as a
kind of absolute being of which individuals are expressions or
reflections, or as a kind of thread of connexion running through
all its members and the same in all of them, we are really dealing
with a conception or general concept which may have logical
meaning, but which cannot be said to be an existent fact along-
side of other existent facts. The unity that belongs to a concept
cannot possibly belong to the mass of individuals to whom the
concept refers.

With a view of bringing together the results of this chapter,
it will be useful to emphasize the following points. In the first
place, we may refer to the distinction already noted between a
particular, definite act of will and a disposition or habit of will

[1] cf. E. Barker, The Discredited State, *Political Quarterly*, 1915.

(i.e. a capacity of willing under suitable circumstances), or systems of such dispositions. Both the particular act of will and the dispositional will are essentially individual, and can never be anything but individual. In the second place, from both of these must be distinguished that which is willed, the object of will. The latter may be individual or common to many acts of will, whether of the same individual or of many individuals. In the third place, from that which is willed we must distinguish that which ought to be willed and which we may call the Good, the nature of which does not consist of being willed and which may or may not, in point of fact, be willed. Now, it might conceivably be proved that the acts of will of individuals and their permanent dispositional wills have a common object, e.g. the maintenance of the social structure. Whether this be so, or not, is a question of fact, and if will involves the presence of a clear idea of the object aimed at, such a will would appear to exist only in the case of a few enlightened individuals. In the case of the majority of people, all that is present is a mild interest, ranging from tacit acquiescence to blank indifference. Further, supposing a will for the maintenance of the social structure be proved to exist in all individuals, it would still be merely a joint will for a common object.

The acts of will, and the systems of dispositions referred to above, need not be, and are not, completely rational or harmonious, either in the individual or in the community. The belief that they are would seem to be due to a confusion between that which is willed and the Good. It is tacitly assumed that that which ought to be willed really is willed by a supposed real self of the individual or by an Absolute Mind. Since that which ought to be willed is presumably rational and harmonious, the real will is conceived as a rational system of purposes, of which particular wills are imperfect manifestations. Here, again, supposing that it could be proved that individual wills are rational and therefore aim at a harmonious good, they would still not constitute a general will, but merely a joint will for the good. The belief that they do constitute a general will is due to a confusion between content and act. Now, acts are always individual

E

and neither the object of will nor the good constitutes existential parts of the individual consciousness, since they are either objects which exist and whose continuance in existence is willed, or else objects which do not exist but which we think ought to exist. In neither case do they form parts of the individual unless the whole distinction between subject and object be invalid. There would seem, therefore, to be no real sense in which unity and continuity can be ascribed to the general will.

In all that has been said, it has not been implied that individuals are isolated beings, independent reals, containing within themselves all that is needed for their development. It is obvious that both for content and mode of experience the individual is largely indebted to the social *milieu*, and that the forces which govern action are products of social connexion and arise from the interaction of personalities in society. But the tissue of psychological forces operating in a society is not unitary in character, though in their highest phases those forces crystallize into unity within unity.[1] In the lowest phases of a people's culture, when conditions are very much alike for all the members, and when there is little or no class differentiation, the members are very homogeneous in character and their feelings, ideas, interests are of a very uniform kind. In the more advanced stages of culture, though at bottom the same essential influences remain to determine the character of all members of a society, and though their common influences are strengthened by the growth of language and the spiritual possessions of a civilized community, yet differentiations take place and we get a number of groupings each with its own atmosphere, moulding the life and action and thought of its members. Individuals may and do belong to more than one of these groupings. Moreover, the latter are in constant motion and transformation and produce collective powers which determine changes in the social, economic and religious life. Some of these collective powers may become crystallized in enduring institutions, but others have only a vague, formless kind of being, and may receive expression in

---

[1] cf. Hobhouse, *Social Evolution and Political Theory*, and G. Schmoller, *Grundriss der Allgemeinen Volkswirtschaftslehre*.

social class-differentiation, political parties, in judgements of value which gradually become standards of conducts, in codes of honour, public opinion. When all this has been admitted, we are yet a long way off the doctrine of an objective mind and will. The tissue of psychological elements referred to has not the kind of being which belongs to a person or self, nor can the kind of influence it exerts on the individual be described as a general will. There need be no mystery about the complex of ideas operating in society and embodied in its institutions, books, laws, etc. Their significance lies in the fact that they are interpreted, modified and sustained by individual minds from generation to generation. Further, the unity which community of ideas gives to associations varies enormously, according to the closeness of the ties that link a member to his group. There is nothing sacrosanct about social organizations. Even states are subject to change and transformation, as recent events show: and as to cultural influences it is surely common experience that individuals often can and do withstand them, abandon, for instance, the language and religion of their race and choose others. No association or associations can ever embrace or exhaust the entire life of man. Men do indeed share in a common life and contribute to a collective achievement, yet nothing but confusion can result from hypostatizing this life and ascribing to it a reality, over and above the reality of the lives which individuals live in relation with one another.

CHAPTER VI

Racial and National Characteristics

WE SAW ABOVE that under the notion of the social mind were
included the mental elements common to the members of a
given people or society, such as common reactions to similar
stimuli, common modes of behaviour due to a similar hereditary structure, and the like. It is these common elements that
are frequently summed up under the name of the 'Soul of a
People', and many writers have used the latter conception to
explain the history of a given people, as though it referred to a
real entity distinct from the generations of individuals that constitute the people and also to account for the differences between
different peoples. In dealing with the problem it is necessary,
to begin with, to distinguish between races and nations. We
cannot here enter into a discussion of the very difficult problem
of the nature of race. Generally the criteria taken by anthropologists are certain bodily characteristics, such as the size and con-
figuration of the head, or colour. But it seems probable that just
as there are somatic types which have been fixed by a long stay
under the same conditions, by heredity and selection, so psychical types of relative permanence may have emerged. It should be
remembered that comparatively little is known with any certainty of psychical racial characteristics, and it is quite possible,
at any rate, that the ultimate differences are not so great as
they are often alleged to be. But granting that there are psychical types corresponding to different races, in what way are these
types to be conceived? Does the existence of a given mental
type involve an appeal to a racial soul immanent in all its members? Such an hypothesis does not appear to be at all required by
the known facts. At least two other ways of conceiving the matter

are possible. We may mean that races differ from one another owing to the fact that *all the members* of a given race possess certain mental qualities, not possessed by any members of other races. These mental qualities would have to be taken as 'fluctuations' in the modern biological sense of the word, i.e. as varying round a mean within given limits; for clearly there are enormous individual differences between the members of a given race. Or, we may mean that all races have the same qualities, but that their distribution varies so that, for instance, certain types of superior ability, though present in all races, are present in greater proportion in some than in others, with the result that the races considered as wholes will differ from one another though individuals of different races may closely resemble one another. Neither of these two possible interpretations of what may be meant by racial types involves or implies the psychical identity of all the members of a race. To appeal to race for the explanation of any psychical factor is in any case dangerous. Remembering the difficulty that anthropologists experience in finding reliable somatic criteria, we ought to be chary of using psychical criteria, until we possess a characterology and a method of record and observation at all comparable in accuracy to, say, craniometry. Further, even where we do find racial psychical peculiarities, we have still the formidable question of deciding how much these are due to heredity and how much to environmental and historical causes. With Professor MacIver we may say that 'in nothing are we more liable to go astray than in the search for the race spirit, if by that we mean a focus of original characters revealed as independent of environment. To find it involves a perilous initial process of abstraction, the almost or altogether impossible process of unravelling the web of life and character woven by the constant infinite reactions of circumstances and the minds of men' (*Community*, p. 148).

A nation we may define provisionally 'as a social group bound together by a consciousness of kind which springs from the traditions evoked by the group's historic past and is directly related to a definite home country'.[1] From the point of view of

[1] Sidney Herbert, *Nationality*, p. 37.

our present discussion it is important to note that two different problems are really involved and have really to be faced. In the first place, there is the problem of the development of the sentiment of nationality, i.e. the consciousness on the part of members of a group that they belong to that group and the gathering of a large number of different emotional dispositions round that group as their object or nucleus. In the second place, we may ask whether there is really such a thing as a distinct national mind or character and what precisely is meant by such phrases.

1. Much has been written of late with regard to the sentiment of nationality and its natural history is now pretty clear. Racial unity is certainly not an essential or necessary condition of national consciousness. Every great nation includes men of different racial stocks. In the British islands, e.g. there are representatives of all the three main races of Europe, the Mediterranean, Alpine and Nordic, and of various sub-races. A classification of the populations of Europe on a racial basis would cut right across national groupings as we know them. Thus, e.g. Normans and Yorkshiremen would form one group, Welsh and Bretons another. Again, direct observation shows that racial unity or community of blood is not essential. The Slav brought up in a Teutonic environment is apt to become a typical German. It may further be readily shown that community of language is neither sufficient nor necessary to the sense of nationality, as is clear from the case of Switzerland, which is trilingual; and Belgium and Canada, which are bilingual. Nor is unity of religion an essential condition. There are many instances where strong patriotism and national cohesion coexist with wide differences in the forms of ecclesiastical administration and profound divergencies in fundamental beliefs; witness England and Germany. Common political allegiance is undoubtedly a strong factor, but there are instances where political union has not promoted national union, as e.g. Ireland, Austria-Hungary and Czarist Russia. All these factors, however, though they are not essential, may be and frequently have been of great importance as contributory causes. But by universal agreement one factor is of fundamental importance, viz. common traditions

and customs, memories of a common past and aspirations for a common future. A nation, says Renan, is a spiritual principle constituted essentially of two things: 'One is the possession in common of a rich legacy of memories; the other is actual consent, the desire to live together, the will to continue to make the best use of the invisible heritage received.' The development of the sense of nationhood is also furthered in some cases by geographical isolation, as is illustrated by the early growth of this sentiment in England and above all by contact and struggle with a foreign foe and resistance to oppression. Thus, to take but a few examples, it was the reaction against English domination that raised the spirit of nationality in France in the fifteenth century; the Dutch became a nation in the struggle against Spain; and in modern times the principle of nationality emerges in its most pronounced form in the Napoleonic Wars. Nationality in the sense here indicated is essentially a sentiment felt by all or the majority of a given social group in varying degrees and consists of a complex of emotional dispositions having for their nucleus or object the group as a whole with all that it stands for, its traditions, ideals and aspirations. The natural history of this sentiment can be traced, the factors that contribute to it enumerated and its biological value in the struggle for existence will be readily appreciated.

2. The second of the problems mentioned above is much more difficult. Rejecting as we have done the conception of a mystical, unitary, social mind, in what sense can we speak of any psychical quality as national and is there such a thing as a *national character*? I think that these terms stand for realities and for purposes of scientific investigation a fairly definite meaning can be attached to them. The psychical qualities 'of a people' are those which are widespread among them, forms of feeling, willing, thinking and acting which are important in the shaping of their behaviour, and characteristic of them in the sense that they enable us to distinguish them from members of other groups. If we so choose we can use at our peril the word soul or mind to indicate the totality of such characteristic and widespread qualities of the members of a people, but we must be

careful to avoid personifying that totality and using it as a principle of explanation wherever everything else fails, to hide our ignorance. Several contributions have been made in recent times to the psychology of peoples, but it is exceedingly difficult to estimate their real scientific value. It is an amusing, but not particularly profitable, task to compare the accounts given by writers of the psychology of peoples other than their own. It would be found, I think, that in many cases the results cancel one another. In particular, it is interesting to notice that nearly all writers claim that their own nation is richest in complexity and variety. A really scientific psychology of peoples will only become possible when we have a developed science of character and have elaborated a reliable system of record and observation. At present differential folk Psychology simply abounds in facile generalizations based on vague impressions of the conduct of a few or on the evidence of selected literary representatives. Nevertheless it would be a mistake to deny the existence of national characteristics. As Steinmetz has said:[1] 'If we assume hereditary racial dispositions and qualities, we are compelled to admit that the dissimilarity of the ways in which races are mixed in different peoples must produce dissimilar national characteristics and that these will be transmissible by heredity. Further great changes must soon take place in such populations, for it is hardly likely that historical events will eliminate or augment the same characteristics in different peoples. In a very short time, a people will, as a result of a different mixture of races in it, exhibit quite different mental and bodily aspects. These peoples can, irrespective of their short duration and of the fact that they contain in the main the same racial elements, come to possess quite different hereditary characteristics. And this happens because of the different way in which social selection acts in the two peoples on the different classes of characteristics and endowments. Difference of habitat, of the international *milieu*, condition a different history, irrespective of race, and this different history causes a different social selection and consequently a

---

[1] 'Der erbliche Rassen- und Volkscharakter', *Vierteljahrschrift fuer Wissensch., Philosophie und Soziologie*, 1902.

different line of transmission and a different national character.' What the qualities constituting such a national character are, it is, as we have seen, exceedingly difficult to determine. We may again quote Steinmetz with advantage: 'We must not imagine that specific qualities like asceticism, cruelty and the like are inherited, nor even the complete dispositions to them. All such qualities are the resultants of various characteristics of the simplest and most general nature, the compounding of which in various proportions and degrees of intensity yields the forms of character as they appear to us with all their secondary features in actual fact. Among the fundamental factors of a given character, there no doubt exists something which *ceteris paribus* will lead its possessor to asceticism. We can picture this something as a pecularity or special degree of rapidity of the course of ideas or presentations, or as a smaller or greater responsiveness of some sense organ or in some analogous manner. The science of character ought to discover the elementary and primary factors of each secondary or resultant quality. Only these elementary factors need to be hereditary to render possible characterological selection. Whoever denies this must assume the absolute equality of all psychical dispositions from primitive man to the West-European.' In addition to the factors of race-mixture, social selection, and heredity, there are also operative the historical occurrences of a people, its tradition and institutions, its system of government and education, group-pressure and suggestion, and these together may be supposed to produce a national type of relative permanence and capable of being transmitted by heredity. Here however we are confronted with the very difficult problem of the relation between innate and acquired characteristics, between nature and nurture and with the problem of the transmission of acquired characteristics. It might be thought, for example, that the effects of institutions and historical happenings generally cannot be permanent, and if national types exist at all they must be due ultimately to original and primary differences. This is a large problem which cannot be discussed here. Perhaps, however, we may say with Stern,[1]

[1] *Differentielle Psychologie*, pp. 27, 69.

'that no sharp separation between innate and acquired qualities is really possible. What is innate is never a quality as such, but merely the indeterminate disposition to it. So, too, what is acquired is never any quality as such; for even a quality which has received its precise form as the result of the strongest action of external factors, must have had some dispositional basis for the external influence to act upon.'

Be this as it may, the conception of a national character does not involve an appeal to a unitary social mind. It does point to the fact that the relation between an individual and his nation is very intimate and organic, that his psychical qualities are due in large measure, both in content and form, to the influence of his nation and its biological and social heritage. But the relation is reciprocal. 'The control exercised by the aggregate over its units tends ever to mould their activities and sentiments and ideas into congruity with social requirements; and these activities, sentiments and ideas, in so far as they are changed by changing circumstances, tend to remould the society into conformity with themselves (Spencer, *Principles of Sociology*, I. 10).

The same is true of the primary qualities above referred to. The inherited dispositions are actualized in a form determined by social experience and under the influence of the environment. Institutions, and traditions in general, mould the behaviour of individuals and determine the way in which the inherited dispositions shall be actualized. But on the other hand tradition and institutions themselves are in the long run due to innate dispositions stimulated to activity by the conditions of the social and physical environment and are constantly modified by the varying circumstances in which individuals find themselves. The national character is thus the complex product of many forces in co-operation. Tradition, social suggestion, race-mixture, social selection, climatic conditions are all contributory causes, the relative share of each of which it is probably impossible to disentangle. But the result that emerges is not a mystical entity hovering over the individuals that constitute a nation, but consists of the totality of certain fundamental psychical characteristics peculiar to and widespread in a certain people, influencing their behaviour, and manifested with greater or less continuity, in a succession of generations. The notion of a *Volksgeist* or national soul in any other sense than this does not seem to be required in social psychology, or to be of any value as a principle of explanation.

CHAPTER VII

Tradition

BY TRADITION IS meant the sum of all the ideas, habits and customs that belong to a people and are transmitted from generation to generation. It has not inaptly been described as the social heritage, for its mode of operation closely resembles that of biological heredity. Like the latter it moulds action and determines behaviour, like the latter it is essentially a principle of continuity, and transmits to future ages the achievements of the past. We have seen that tradition is an essential factor in the development of the sentiment of nationality, and also in the actual moulding of national types. Perhaps its importance can be exhibited by contrasting the life of peoples with a long traditional past with those among whom no steady tradition has yet developed. The Russian philosopher, Chaadaev, thinks that the Russian people are essentially lacking in this force of tradition, and that this lack constitutes a real weakness in their national character, and accounts for their relative mental and even physical instability. The following passage, which I translate from a quotation given in Dr Elias Hurwicz's *Die Seelen der Völker*, will make the point clear: 'What is human life, if the recollections of former events do not link the present with the past (Cicero). We others, however, like illegitimate children without a patrimony, without anything to link us up with the men who lived before us, retain in our minds none of the teachings of the past. Each one of us is compelled to pick up anew the torn threads of his relationships. What to other people has become habitual and instinctive has to be knocked into our heads with hammer blows. Our memory does not go beyond yesterday: we are, so to speak, strangers to ourselves. We move

in so strange a manner that with every step in a forward direction, the past moment has irretrievably disappeared. This is the
natural consequence of a culture based on borrowed elements
and on imitation. We do not pursue a course of development
from within, we do not progress naturally: each new idea drives
away the old without leaving a trace, since it is not derived from
them, but comes to us God knows whence. Since we only
receive ready-made ideas, there are not formed in our brains
those permanent paths which make possible a gradual development. We grow but do not mature, we move forward but in a
directionless line. We are like children who have not been
taught to think for themselves; in the period of their maturity it
becomes evident that they have nothing of their own, that all
that they know lies on the surface of their being, that their soul
is outside them. This is the case with us. It is easy to see that this
strange fate of a people – which was not able to link up its
thoughts in a slowly evolving chain, and which has only taken
part in the general evolution of the human spirit through blind,
superficial, and often unsuccessful imitation – was bound to
have a powerful effect on the mentality of each of its individual
members. Consequently you will find that we are all lacking in
confidence, method, logic. It is natural to man to lose his grip of
things, when he finds no means to link him with the past and
future. He loses all stability and confidence. Without the
guidance of the feeling of continuity, he is lost in the world.
Such "uprooted" men one can meet in all countries; with us,
however, they are a common phenomenon. This has nothing to
do with the lightness of spirit, with which the French were
once reproached, and which at bottom was nothing but an
ability for rapid adaptation which was not incompatible with
width and depth, and which lent charm and elegance to human
intercourse; rather is it the recklessness of a life, lacking in
experience and foresight, and taking nothing into consideration
but the ephemeral existence of an individual torn from his kind.
In our minds there is nothing common; everything therein is
isolated, unstable and incomplete. Indeed, we find in our
gaze something vague, cold and indeterminate, reminding us

somewhat of the physiognomy of peoples who belong to the lowest scale of the social ladder.' More recently, Isgojew has shown the influence of this relative absence of tradition upon the Russian youth, and it is possible that in it is to be found one of the main causes of the present state of affairs in Russia.

The mode in which intellectual tradition operates, through books, systems of education, etc., is fairly familiar, and will not be discussed here. It is proposed to confine attention mainly to custom and to deal briefly with its relation to law and morals.

Wundt defines custom as a form of voluntary action that has been developed in a national or tribal community. Psychologically, custom in some respects resembles habit; i.e. custom is habit that is followed not only by one individual, but by the majority of a community. Custom, however, is by no means identical with habit. The former involves a rule or norm, and has an obligatory character. The term rule is intended to bring out two important features of custom, viz. (i) that custom is not merely a prevailing habit of action or behaviour, but implies a judgement upon action or behaviour; and (ii) that this judgement is general and impersonal in its terms. The obligatory character of custom enables us to distinguish it from usage. The latter consists of those actions habitual to members of a community, which do not possess normative character or lack the sanction of moral constraint. Custom can thus be distinguished from habit by its universal and normative character, and from usage chiefly by the latter characteristic. Custom, in other words, is *sanctioned* usage.

Custom has further to be distinguished from fashion. It is sometimes said that fashion is simultaneous conformity in action; i.e. under its influence each person does what every one else is doing, and is thus based on imitation; while custom is successive conformity: in other words, when acting in accordance with custom, each person does what has always been done, and it is thus based essentially on habit. But there are more important distinguishing features. In the first place, custom seems to be concerned with constant and fundamental needs of society, while fashion or vogue seems to affect less vital and less general spheres of life. Fashion is essentially evanescent and changeable. It is in fact a series of recurring changes, often marked by rhythmic imitation and innovation. Custom, on the other hand, is essentially enduring and continuous, and subject only to slow change. Of course there are some fashions that do not change, but in so far as that is the case, they have really passed into custom; in other words, they have the prestige of the past as well as that of the present. In the second place, there would appear to be a total difference of motive between custom and fashion. Neither can be adequately characterized by mere uniformity of action, because there are many uniform actions based on instinct or hereditary structure generally. But whilst custom is followed because it has generally been followed in the past, fashion is followed because it is now generally followed. Further, in a sense fashion makes for novelty, and its essential basis is to be found in the passion for self-individualization or differentiation. Custom, on the other hand, owes much of its force to the fact that through it society has warded off the dangers of novelty. Thus 'custom' imitation and 'mode' imitation work in different directions. The one tends to perpetuate and stereotype the old; the other to bring in innovations and to spread them by imitation.

The Origin of Custom. – Wundt tells us that 'custom has, as far as we know, but one course of development, and that is from preceding custom of kindred context. Usage, fashion, and habits, on the other hand, constitute a mixed medley of new forms and relics of a long dead past. Transmission and new formation are here often enough difficult of discrimination, but there is no such thing as an entirely new custom'. This is true in the sense that custom is a common creation, the result of a thousand manifold interactions. But it must not be taken as implying the existence of a supermind or common self of society. In the last resort, custom must be due to some individual habit meeting other individual habits, their constant modification each by the other, and eventual crystallization into a composite resultant. After all, society is, as Professor Hobhouse says,[1] ourselves and those not so greatly differing from us who came before us, and custom must have grown up in the past in much the same way as it does now. What happens now is that opinions or judgements radiate from some individual centre, impinge on the opinions of others, clash with or reinforce them, modify or are modified by them, and eventually out of the clash of ideas and influences there emerges a more or less stable opinion or judgement which will henceforth act as an influence to mould the ideas of other men. Always we have individual centres living and developing in a social environment, modifying and being modified by that environment. The ideas and general rules of action or behaviour that emerge in society are due to individual minds in inter-relation, and there need be no mystery about the nature of the social process involved in their evolution. The same factors must have been operative in primitive society, except that new ideas would have had a smaller chance of survival over against the tremendous force of the past, and their spread by imitation or discussion must have been more difficult, owing to the poverty in means of communication.

Wundt thinks all customary acts were in their origin acts of worship. For this there does not appear to be any satisfactory evidence; but there can be no doubt that custom was held to be divinely sanctioned.

The Function of Custom. – According to the theory of natural selection, it is held that reflex actions and instinctive acts have been selected out of the random and sporadic movements which are to be observed in all living things, and perpetuated owing to their value in the struggle for existence. The importance of instincts, in particular, lies in the fact that by their means an animal can go through a complicated series of acts without having to reason about each step or to grasp the real end of the series as a whole. Hereditary structure thus enables an organism to deal with a complicated situation effectively, and independently of its own individual experience, and is thus one way in which the race operates upon the individual. The human being, like other animals, is endowed with inherited modes of be-

[1] *Morals in Evolution*, p. 13.

haviour, though in his case the instincts do not survive in isolation, but are fused with one another and profoundly modified, at any rate, in the mode and manner of their realization or expression, by experience. In the case of human beings, however, the race operates on the individual also, by means of tradition or custom; i.e. by perpetuating or transmitting those modes of action which the experience of past generations has proved to be beneficial. In this way, it has the effect of saving new generations from having to re-learn by a costly process of trial and error what has already been learnt by former generations. It is this function of custom which is dwelt upon when it is described as social heredity. It resembles instinctive and inherited modes of action in that the modes of behaviour which custom prescribes are (i) due to the race (ii) can be and generally are performed without any reasoning process, and (iii) are generally, or have been originally, useful to the members of society. In regard to the latter point, it should be remembered that even instincts are occasionally injurious, and certainly many customs outlive their real function and become atrophied and thus constitute a real danger to society. But in their origin they must have become 'stamped in', owing to their utility or survival value.

The Power of Custom. – The great influence of custom has frequently been emphasized in literature. Thus Shakespeare speaks of 'tyrant custom'; Montaigne calls it a 'violent and treacherous schoolmistress'; according to Bacon it is 'the principal magistrate of man's life,' and Locke ascribes to it 'greater power than nature.'[1] Certainly in primitive societies custom permeates all spheres of life and prescribes the minutest details of conduct; and among civilized peoples the sway of custom and fashion is greater than is commonly realized. Ultimately the power of custom is due, in all probability, to the biological utility of uniformity of action. In early phases of social evolution, it must have been, as Bagehot points out, of tremendous importance that some general rules should be established which should bind men together, make them do much the same things,

[1] cf. Ross, *Social Control*, p. 184.

tell them what to expect of each other. No doubt, too, it is largely because men instinctively feel the importance of custom that a semi-supernatural sanction was attached to it, and departure or deviation from it severely punished.[Psychologically the force of custom is often ascribed to habit and suggestion.] But such generalities explain very little. The force of suggestion is due to an appeal to some emotional and instinctive tendencies, the arousing of which tends to inhibit all conflicting ideas and to maintain the suggested idea in the focus of attention and to give it dynamic energy. It is therefore necessary, as Hart has shown, to point in each case to the particular tendencies involved. Possibly the suggestive force of custom is due to the herd instinct. Trotter has shown that everything that comes to us from the herd has enormous prestige. There appears to be also involved a sort of fear of the unknown in the dislike of change, which is the other side, so to speak, of the love of the familiar and old. There may be something elemental in this. Certainly one of the strongest characteristics of primitive man is his fear of the unknown. He is constantly in dread lest some action of his should bring upon him the anger of the gods. The uniform and constant comes to be understood and anticipated. The new and varied cannot be relied upon, cannot be calculated in advance, and is therefore full of terrors. In the customary, in what has always been done, there is safety. Hence the reverence for custom, and the horror of innovation. Primitive man therefore surrounds his customs with an air of sanctity and punishes severely any violation of them. When supernatural sanction fails, men find other sanctions, and even invent pseudo-scientific justifications for the reign of the old and familiar. 'One of the greatest pains to a human nature,' says Bagehot, 'is the pain of a new idea. It is, as common people say, so "upsetting"; it makes you think that after all your favourite notions may be wrong, your firmest beliefs ill-founded.' Even when changes are introduced, often their only chance of success is to come in the guise of old customs. Maine has drawn attention to many such fictions in primitive law, and many examples could be given from quarters nearer home. An illustration of the same tendency can be seen in the fact that many customs persist long after their original cause has ceased to be operative. In many cases elaborate rationalizations are then invented to account for them, and reasons are then assigned to them which have little or nothing to do with their original significance. Andrew Lang pointed out that myths are frequently invented to account for striking customs.

Custom and Law. – The connexion between custom and law has been much emphasized by the historical school of jurisprudence. Among primitive peoples certainly, custom stands for law, and much of the modern systems of law is based on ancient custom. Westermarck points out that laws themselves frequently command obedience more as customs than as laws. Often, in competition with law, custom carries the day, and frequently, when a custom cannot abrogate the law, it exercises a paralysing influence on the execution of the latter; compare the attitude to duels on the Continent. So too, contrary to law, the sentence of death in some European countries is not carried into execution. Custom resembles law in its obligatory character, and in the fact that, like law, it is concerned with externals and only to a limited extent with motives. Its resemblance to law should bring out the important fact that custom cannot be due to mere mechanical repetition, but does in fact express a judgement, and implies in its origin a conscious sense of right and wrong. Customary rules are thus the expression of popular conceptions, however rudimentary and dim, of right and wrong (see Vinogradoff, *Common Sense in Law*, Ch. on 'Custom').

The terms, ethics, morality, *Sittlichkeit* all indicate the close connexion between morality and custom. The development of morality, historically speaking, consists largely in the attempt to find a rational basis of conduct, to criticize and if necessary to re-model the rules of conduct prescribed by custom. It hardly needs to be pointed out that this process is far from complete, and that much of our present-day morality is merely traditional and conventional, and has not yet reached the reflective stage. Westermarck points out that there may exist customary modes of action, i.e. actions which are generally prevalent and which are yet morally condemned. But it is doubtful in such cases whether the moral condemnation or reprobation is either genuine or profound: so that custom is a very good index of the real moral sense of a people. Custom, however, does not cover the whole field of morality, because, like law, it deals mainly with externals.

It follows from what has been said that both custom and law are in a way the expression of the growing moral sense of a community. This fact has been used in support of the theory of a national mind or soul. In regard to law in particular, the so-called Historical School maintains that law is the product of a people's genius manifesting itself in all the members of a people and is not due to the deliberate will of a legislator. The function of the latter is not on this view to create new rules but to declare an existing state of legal consciousness. The historical school of jurisprudence was one of the manifestations of the romantic movement and developed largely in reaction against the intellectualism of the eighteenth century. But the notion of a *Volksgeist* was conceived by the writers of the school in a vague and abstract manner, and in any case it has not proved a fertile idea as far as the history of law is concerned. One of the pupils of Savigny, who was the founder of this school (Puchta, 1798–1846), certainly personifies the popular mind and regards it as an entity independent of the individual consciousness. It is not even a product of the historic life of a people, but exists from the beginning of a people's historical evolution and determines both the customs and history of the people. It must be obvious that as a principle of explanation, such a notion cannot be helpful and is bound to result in purely circular arguments; the soul of a people can only be known through its manifestations, yet the manifestations are caused by the soul. It should be noted further that in the majority of cases this objectification or personification of the soul of a people has led the followers of the school to deny the validity of international law, for although there are national souls there is no such thing as the soul of humanity, and consequently there can be no law binding humanity as a whole. On the whole movement it will be well perhaps to quote the authoritative statement of Professor Vinogradoff.[1] 'The mystic nationalism of the Romantic theory has not stood the test of critical examination and of scientific progress. Nations are live beings in a certain sense, but not in the same sense as individuals. They are not circumscribed to the same extent in their development by unyielding forms, they react more freely against circumstances and command a wider range of adaptation. . . . Ihering has shown that the progress of law is not merely the result of an unconscious growth conditioned by innate character and environment, but also the result of conscious endeavour to solve the problems of social existence. . . . While in early periods legal rules grow more or less organically like language and myth, later stages are characterized by universal and as it were impersonal concepts which like coins of standard make circulate without difficulty through the world.'

The historical school of jurisprudence was to some extent influenced by Hegel, but his theory, particularly in the form it has assumed in his English followers, is capable of being stated in a way which would be quite compatible with the statement just quoted from Professor Vinogradoff. The general will is according to this view essentially rational; it is in fact identical with the rational will, and law is regarded as an expression of this rational will. Now in a sense this is true, for law and custom do embody a gradually developing sense of right and wrong. But it seems mistaken to regard the will of the people as a single and unitary entity. Actual laws are the results of many minds in interaction and the element of rationality in them must not be exaggerated. What is really behind the theory of law as an expression of a general will, is the difficulty of accounting for the fact of obligation. It seems natural to argue that the feeling of obligation on the part of an individual to obey a law can only be explained by showing that he himself 'really' wills that law, though 'actually' at the moment it may be repugnant to him, that he recognizes the necessity of the law in general though he finds it hard in his own case. But here two problems are really confused. We must distinguish clearly the problem of the origin of the

[1] *Historical Jurisprudence*, vol. i, p. 134.

sense or feeling of obligation from the problem of the logical
basis or justification of obligation. The former, as a matter of
psychological history, is probably largely due to the fact that law
and custom come to the individual from without and carry with
them the prestige of the community whose will they are supposed to express. But the logical basis of obligation cannot be
found in the mere fact of willing, whether on the part of the
community, or the individual. The mere fact that the community wills or that I myself will that a certain thing should be,
is no reason why it ought to be. Obligation cannot consist in
being willed as a mere psychological fact. Its basis must lie in an
objective moral order rationally determinable, but such an
objective moral order is not in any sense dependent upon being
willed any more than an object known consists in its being
known. Actual law of course only approximates to this objective
moral order. Many systems of law contain elements which
though people may in point of fact feel obliged to obey them
are not rationally justifiable. The theory of a general will therefore really obscures the facts, and it is moreover open to the
objection that like the theory of the historical school in general,
it lends itself to a narrow and exclusive nationalism. It is also,
as we have seen, essentially conservative and leads to a glorifica-
tion of the *status quo*. But both the historical development of law
and its ethical justification can be stated in terms which do not
imply a general will in the sense of a unitary entity. 'All wills,'
we may say with Duguit,[1] 'are individual wills; all are equivalent
in value; there is no hierarchy of wills. All wills are equal if one
considers the subject only. Their value can be determined only
by the end which they pursue. The will of those who govern
has no force as such; it has value and force only to the extent that
it makes for the organization and functioning of a public service.'

---

[1] *Law and the State*, p. 184.

CHAPTER VIII

Community, Associations and Institutions

THE PROBLEM OF the nature of community raises fundamental questions in Ethics, Sociology, Jurisprudence, Political
Science and Metaphysics, and is thus extremely complicated.
What is the relation between individual and society? What is
the community? Is it a mere collection, or has it a unity comparable to the unity of an organism or person? What is the
nature of social groupings within community, or what is their
relation to the whole? Has community as such ends of its own,
or does it exist merely to render possible the realization of the
ends of the individuals that compose it? Is there any real meaning in this contrast, or is it perhaps based on false abstractions?
These and other questions press for an answer, particularly at
present, in view of the emergence into power of strong groups
within community challenging the omnipotence and omnicom-
petence of the State and claiming a readjustment of their
relations to the general community. Most of these problems,
however, centre in the question of the nature of community.
The answers to that question have been numerous, but until
recently the prevailing doctrine regarding the nature of the
social reality has been the organic theory. We need not here
enter into a detailed account of the various ways in which the
latter conception has been worked out, nor to point again to the
ludicrous extremes to which some writers have pushed the
analogy between community and organism. The theory, at its
best, does bring out some important points which may be briefly
summarized. Firstly, it rightly insists that individuals in society

are essentially and intrinsically connected, and that the social whole is constituted by their inter-relations. In this respect [society is organic,] not in the sense that it is like an animal or a vegetable, but rather in the sense that it satisfies the definition of the organic in the wider sense as consisting of a 'whole constituted by the interconnection of parts which are themselves maintained each by its interconnection with the remainder' (Hobhouse). In the second place, the theory rightly emphasized the fact that [community is not a mechanical or artificial device or construction, but a living thing and a natural growth. In this respect, too, societies are not really like other organisms, for instance, they do not grow or reproduce themselves or die like organisms.] Nevertheless, they do exhibit something of the organic character in adaptability to environment and plasticity of adjustment, and they certainly are not mechanical or accidental aggregates. In the third place, it followed from the organic theory that radical and sudden transformations of society are difficult,[1] and that it is dangerous to deal with social questions in isolation – that the inter-relations of social affairs are so close that no part of the social problem can be dealt with without affecting the rest.

These are the elements of value in the theory, but the danger of it lies in the fact that it leads people to exaggerate the unity of actual communities which approximate to the organic in varying degrees. Not only so, but even taking the most highly developed communities, the organic theory does not rightly represent the relation of the individual to the community. The latter is infinitely complex and contains unity within unity, group within group, in enormous variety, and the relations of the individual to his group differ in different cases, according to the interests which they represent or stand for. Further, the organic theory ignores the elements of conflict and disharmony which abound in community. There is in a sense a common life, and the community seeks to maintain itself as a whole, but the unity attained is often won not by the liberation of living energy, but by

---

[1] Note, however, that the theory of mutations has been used by some to justify revolutions.

mechanical suppression and repression, and the 'life of the community' may in fact mean the life of a very small dominant section of it. Above all, the organic theory obscures the fact that the individual, though essentially related to the community – the community is nothing but individuals in relation – is not exhausted in those relations, that he is a unique centre of consciousness which is not fused with the life of the whole.

The organic theory has also been expressed in psychological terms. Community has been described as a mind or person. The latter theory has already been discussed, and we have seen reason for rejecting it as inadequate and misleading. Fundamentally, all over-individual theories of community are open to the objection that unconsciously they tend to personify community and to look at its life as other than the life of its members in relation with one another, and to ascribe to it ends which are not the ends of the individuals composing it. Now we certainly do often attribute personality to groups or communities in the sense that they evoke in us interest and emotions analogous to the interests and emotions which persons evoke in us. Again, for legal and moral purposes groups are often treated as persons or subjects of rights and duties. But these facts do not present any real theoretical difficulty. One fails to see why collective bodies should cease to be responsible for their actions, or fail to evoke interest and emotion. The problem of the ends of community, as compared with the ends of the individuals composing it, is more difficult. [All values are values for persons, and must consist in something intrinsic to personality. But, of course, the interests of personality are essentially largely social in character, and the good of the individual properly understood is the good of society. The latter must indeed be something that is realized or attained by the individuals composing it and, on the other hand, the ends of individuals must embrace the harmonious development of all individuals in society, since these ends, ethically speaking, are essentially social in character.] This point, however, raises difficult problems in ethics which cannot here be discussed. This much we do learn from the organic theory, namely that the relations between individuals are essential and intrinsic to their personality, but it should be remembered that these relations are of various kinds, that they are not all equally vital, and they contain elements of conflict as well as of harmony. Community is not a mere collection, but neither is it a mind or person. There is in it a nisus towards unity, but the unity, even when attained, will not be adequately described in terms of the relations that bind part to part in an organism or person, but will be a relational unity of a more complex kind.

In recent treatments of this subject, important contributions have been made to the clarification of our theory of society and, incidentally, towards a scientific terminology.[1] It is important to distinguish between Community and Association, and to determine the precise relation between associations and institutions. By Community is to be understood a group of social beings living a common life, including all the infinite variety and complexity of relations which result from that common life or constitute it. It is obvious that there are many relations between human beings which escape formal organization either because they are so subtle and delicate that they cannot be confined within more or less mechanical modes of arrangement, or because they are so simple that they do not need it. The relations are essentially psychical in character, but they are so varied and multitudinous, convergent but also divergent, that they do not constitute a unity. Further, even in community, the individual is not exhausted. Though he needs it for his development and much of his mental content is made up actually of his relations to others, his affections, likes and dislikes, his duties and obligations, yet there is a core of being in him which is unique and incommunicable. Though he enters into relations, he is therefore not exhausted in these relations.

By Association we mean a group of social beings related to one another by the fact that they possess or have instituted in common an organization, with a view to securing a specific end or specific ends.

Associations are partial forms of community. While the latter embraces all the interests and relations between men, whether

[1] See MacIver, *Community*, and G. D. H. Cole, *Social Theory*.

organized or not, associations rest on specific purposes, they exist to fulfil some definite end. They vary in scope, comprehensiveness and permanence in accordance with the scope, comprehensiveness and permanence of the purposes for which they exist. It is not intended to imply that all associations have come about deliberately and are based on conscious purpose. This is obviously not the case. They arise often as the result of dimly felt needs and pressure of circumstances, grope their way for a long time, perhaps, without finding their real purpose, but purposive they all are in nature, i.e. they cannot be understood without reference to the end which they subserve, though that end may not be fully realized by all or even the majority of the members of the association.

Institutions are definite and sanctioned forms or modes of relationship between social beings, in respect to one another or to some external object. Associations, we have seen, imply and depend on organization. If several people are to co-operate in the execution of a common task, there must be division of labour, rules of procedure and the like. In other words, the relations between the individuals of the association must be defined and receive a common sanction. This happens whenever the association has a certain permanence and rests on ends which are of vital importance. In this way there arise customs and laws, rules of procedure, systems of work which we call institutions. The associations are living things and consist of individual persons working together for common ends; the institutions it would be better to regard as forms of relation between them, ways of action among associated individuals which have received social sanction. Institutions are often identified with associations, but it would be conducive to clearness if the terms were kept distinct. We also often speak of buildings as institutions, but in such cases we really mean to refer to the external embodiment or instrument of the institution.

Associations create and sustain institutions, while the latter in turn react upon the associations. Occasionally, there are cases in which institutions appear to give rise to associations, e.g. war may lead to the formation of an army (Hetherington and

Muirhead). But these cases require further analysis. War is an institution in the sense that it is a recognized method of settling disputes of a certain character between the associations we call States. It is really these associations that create armies, i.e. more limited associations in order to achieve the ends which the war is entered into. Institutions are always definite forms of social relationship – but sometimes they are immediately related to a clearly defined association, at other times they are embodied in some form of social behaviour related to some very general association.[1]

Associations and institutions, even when they are not called into being by a definite act of will, always have the character, as Professor Bosanquet urges,[2] that they appear *as if* they had been instituted to fulfil some purpose. Institutions have therefore been spoken of as the meeting-point of wills, as objectified purposes, the embodiment in external form of an end which some group of individuals has proposed to itself. This requires very careful qualifications. In the first place, though institutions can only be understood teleologically, yet we must not impute clear or conscious purpose to the individuals of the associations sustaining them or to the associations as wholes, any more than we can impute conscious purposes to the lower animals capable of conative behaviour. In the second place, we are not entitled to assume unity of purpose. Institutions are ways which society has come to recognize as meeting certain demands, and as enabling associations to continue in existence and to secure co-operation. In all institutions there is therefore a social element, but it must be remembered that they are never the result of a single mind, and do not as a rule embody clearly conceived rational purposes. They are the meeting-point of many minds, and the result of the clash between idea and idea, will and will; and therefore contain within themselves elements of selfishness, of vanity, of cruelty, as well as of self-sacrifice, devotion and human kindness. The rational element in institutions must, therefore, not be exag-

[1] It should be noted that institutions are offshoots of community as well as of association.

[2] *Philosophical Theory of the State*, p. 297.

gerated, and it is of the utmost importance that they should be constantly criticised with a view of determining what purposes they really embody, and whether their purposes are worthy of our devotion and energy. War is an institution, but he would be a bold man who would urge that it is the embodiment of a rational purpose and an ethical idea. Or consider the modern wage system; it came into being gradually on the disappearance of slavery and serfdom, but the purposes which it fulfils are not harmonious and have never been clearly thought out. The same is true of any other complex institution. Again, the purposes underlying an institution are not at all, in most cases, identical for all its members. The institution of the wage-system cannot mean the same thing to the factory worker as it means to the factory owner; nor the institution of slavery to the slave as to the slave owner.

Institutions then are not the embodiment of a unitary mind, but the results of thousands of minds in inter-relation. They do not as a rule embody clearly conceived purposes, but are much more accurately described as trial and error experiments which grow up in a groping way as the results of the efforts of individual social beings to find a *modus vivendi* and which receive social sanction when found more or less to meet the needs of life. In particular it should be noticed that even when the relation of some individuals to a given institution is conscious and deliberate, the inter-relation between individual minds, the degree of their opposition and co-operation, is not, except in the most advanced stages, guided by any clear mind, and to this is to be ascribed the incoherence of many institutions.

These considerations are important when we come to deal with the relations between individuals and institutions.

(*a*) It is sometimes maintained that all institutions are a dead-weight, a hindrance to the free development of the spirit, and that the complexity and number of associations of modern life are mechanizing the individual. This argument is probably at bottom due to a confused idea of the relation between mechanism and purpose. It can I think be shown that purposive action does not exclude but in fact rests upon mechanism. The criticism is however of value in so far as it warns us against the tendency of institutions to atrophy and lose their vitality.

(b) Sometimes it is maintained that institutions relating to material things and changes in them can have no effect at all on the human spirit and that for any genuine reform it is the latter that must be changed. Compare Aristotle's argument against Plato's communism. 'Of course evils disfigure the State, but they do not spring from natural things like property. These evils are due to the wickedness of human nature. (11.5.12.) It is not the possessions but the desires of mankind that require to be equalized. (11.7.8.)' We must use spiritual means, such as education, custom and laws, philosophy; and he expresses surprise that Plato, who attached so much importance to education, should have recourse to regulations of the sort. (11.5.15.) In reality, however, spirit cannot be divorced from matter and the forms of life have a tremendous influence on life itself. Apart from institutions, the individual would remain a bare potentiality, and the direction of his development and the actual content of his mind are determined very largely by his social relationships. The relation between institutions and human potentialities is to this extent organic that the actual form of the realization of the latter depends upon the former.

(c) It follows that it is quite false to maintain that 'human nature cannot be altered'. Human nature, on the contrary, is malleable and changes in its concrete manifestations with changes in social circumstances and institutions. With the same native dispositions people will behave differently under different circumstances.[1] 'A Dutchman has probably much the same native disposition as a German, but his instincts in adult life are very different owing to the absence of militarism and of the pride of a Great Power. It is obvious that the instincts of celibates become profoundly different from those of other men and women. Almost any instinct is capable of many different forms according to the nature of the outlets which it finds. The same

---

[1] There is very little evidence of change in congenital tendencies, but in regard to the mode of realization of inherited tendencies, human nature appears to be malleable.

instinct which leads to artistic or intellectual creativeness may under other circumstances lead to a love of war' (B. Russell, *Principles of Social Reconstruction*, p. 40).

(*d*) Although institutions are thus integral elements of human development and are organically related to human potentialities, yet it does not follow that the relation of the individual to them must on that account be of enthusiastic adoration and submission. Though institutions are necessary to human life and arise out of the needs of life, it is never safe to argue that any particular form of a given institution is essential to personality and therefore sacrosanct. This has been urged on behalf of private property, the State, the Churches, armies and navies, etc. No doubt they arise in response to some need, but having arisen they have a tendency to resist change and resent criticism and thus to become oppressive and a hindrance to life and free development. All institutions must be judged by the degree in which they render possible the realization of personality, and an effective criticism of them is impossible if we begin by assuming that institutions as we find them are essential to personality. Thus, though it may well be maintained that some form of property or of the power of more or less exclusive control over things is necessary to self-realization, it must not be assumed on that account that the particular form of property which happens to prevail now is essential. It is in fact easy to show that the present form of private property, and in particular the love of money which it encourages, cramps many lives and hinders their development. Many other cases could easily be adduced to a like effect. If then we wish to speak of institutions as objectified purposes at all, we must add that these purposes are not clearly apprehended and that they are often conflicting and inharmonious.

Associations as we have seen exist in order to fulfil certain purposes and there are as many distinct associations as there are specific social purposes. Each expresses or embodies a partial interest of the individual and therefore of the community, but some associations are very comprehensive owing to the fact that they rest on interests which affect a large number of people, or

even like the State, all the members of a society. All the associations taken together or the whole associational structure may
be described as society,[1] but society is not identical with community since the latter includes relationships that do not receive
form or embodiment in associations or institutions. The relation between the individual and community is therefore the
most intimate and close. His relation to associations will vary.
The philosopher may not be interested at all in an association of
philatelists and may be only vaguely interested in the Church or
the Trade Unions, etc. In any case all the associational relations
taken together do not exhaust his individuality, firstly, because
behind society stands the community with the infinitely subtle
relations that characterize it, and secondly, because even community still leaves a core of individuality which is not communicable.

[1] Professor Hobhouse would make 'society' the widest term.

CHAPTER IX

The Psychology of the Crowd

HAVING CONSIDERED the general character of community in relation to the social individuals that constitute it, we may now proceed to examine the psychological characteristics of minor social aggregates, such as crowds, mobs, organized bodies. I will deal first with the so-called 'psychology of the crowd'. There exists now quite a large number of works dealing with the subject, but the words of Professor Graham Wallas in his 'Great Society' remain true, that the whole subject requires re-statement and re-examination. In particular much confusion has arisen from the use of collective terms and from a lack of accurate classification and designation of different kinds of social aggregates. Le Bon, whose work is very widely read, uses the term crowd in a very wide sense, so that, for instance, the 'era of crowds' and the 'rule of the masses' are interchangeable terms. Physical presence is not in his view necessary to constitute a 'psychological crowd'. The essential requisite apparently is the turning of the feelings and ideas of a number of people, in an identical direction, and the consequent formation, according to him, of a kind of unitary collective mind.

Sir Martin Conway[1] also uses the term crowd to cover any group of human beings that have a separate and conscious existence and to include such widely divergent collectivities as mobs, public meetings, the race, the empire, the nation. Tarde has drawn a useful distinction between the crowd and the public. There is certainly a great need for a preliminary

[1] *The Crowd in Peace and War.*

F

classification of social wholes, if we are to escape the danger of sweeping generalizations.

We may to begin with divide social aggregates into organized and unorganized. (This is of course a matter of degree only; for even a very temporary crowd develops some kind of organization.) The latter can be conveniently divided into those aggregations that are dependent on physical presence or contact, namely, crowds and mobs, and those that are not primarily dependent on physical contact, which we may call the Public. The organized aggregates include all sorts of associations, i.e. aggregations of individuals that have a relatively stable organization, with relatively developed forms of collective action and thought. It is much to be regretted that the psychology of these latter has not received the same attention that has been given to the mental phenomena of crowds and mobs.

We may first consider assemblages or aggregations characterized by physical presence or contact. These include crowds and mobs, the latter being a sub-species of the former and characterized essentially by instability and disorder. What then is a crowd? To begin with there must be a common direction of attention. A mass of people each going on his own business is not a crowd. There is needed a common object of interest arousing similar ideas and emotions in the minds of each individual constituting the crowd. In addition there generally supervenes a kind of feeling of the 'presence' of others and a realization that one's ideas and emotions are shared by others. These characteristics imply and depend upon a certain homogeneity in the constituent members. To be attracted by the same object of interest, people must have a good deal in common.

Descriptions of crowds all emphasize these facts, though the conclusions they draw from them vary. For example, we hear of 'strained attention', 'feeling of expectancy', 'a narrowing of consciousness' and of phenomena usually accompanying concentrated attention, such as deep silence and bated breath. Compare the following account of a Paderewski *Matinée*. 'There is a chatter, a rustling of programmes, a waving of fans, a nodding of feathers, a general air of expectancy and the lights are lowered. A hush. All eyes are turned to a small door leading on to the stage; it is opened. Paderewski enters. A storm of applause greets him, but after it comes a tremulous hush and a prolonged sigh, created by the long deep inhalation of upward of three thousand women. Paderewski is at the piano. Thousands of eyes watch every commonplace movement (of his) through opera glasses with an intensity painful to observe. He the idol, they the idolators. Towards the end of the performance, the most decorous women seem to abandon themselves to the influence. There are sighs, sobs, the tight clenching of the palms, the bowing of the head. Fervid exclamations, "He is my master!" are heard in the feminine mob' (Sidis, *Psychology of Suggestion*, 301, quoted Ross, *Social Psychology*, p. 45).

Both in antiquity and in modern times much has been made of the low degree of intelligence exhibited by crowds, and even of assemblies such as Senates and Parliaments. 'You can talk a mob into anything; its feelings may be – usually are – on the whole generous and right; but it has no foundation for them, no hold of them; you may tease or tickle it into any, at your pleasure; it thinks by infection, for the most part, catching a passion like a cold, and there is nothing so little that it will not roar itself wild about, when the fit is on; nothing so great but it will forget in an hour, when the fit is past' (Ruskin, *Sesame*, p. 26).[1]

Much mystery has been made of this fact, but it appears capable of a very simple explanation. Collective deliberation can only yield good results when there is a genuine interchange of views and when each member is able to throw some light on the problem under discussion based on his own observation. This leads to genuine integrative and co-operative thinking which can produce results superior to anything any individual could have produced by himself. In unorganized crowds such free interchange is impossible. The majority are bound to be passive

[1] cf. Schiller:

Jeder, siehst du ihn einzeln is leidlich klug und verständig, Sind sie *in corpore*, gleich wird dir ein Dummkopf daraus.

listeners and consequently the influence of the few who generally know something of mass psychology is predominant. The leader who wants to convince a crowd will obviously not use arguments which could appeal only to a few highly trained logical thinkers, but will have recourse to simple analogies, facile generalizations, appeals to emotions, etc. which will be effective as far as the majority is concerned. It is obvious that the ideas which can be understood by all or the majority of a crowd will be of a low order and therefore collective thinking of unorganized assemblages must be of a low level. In particular when a crowd is under the influence of an orator, collective thinking often vanishes to a minimum. There is not the give and take of conversation. 'The life of a conversation is gone the moment one individual takes the floor and silences the rest. I believe it was the poet Rogers who wittily said that the number at a dinner party should be less than the Muses and more than the Graces. Where more than nine people are assembled about a table the danger of crowd formation arises. Three or less are not a party at all' (Sir Martin Conway, p. 22).

The crowd cannot think collectively. It can only listen to competing leaders and follow one of them.

Added to the fact that only rudimentary arguments can appeal to *all* the members of a crowd, is the heightening of the suggestibility of its members. Arguments that come to the individual with the prestige of the crowd are accepted more readily than they would be if listened to in isolation. The essence of suggestion is the inhibition of ideas other than the one in the focus of consciousness and the coming into play of some emotional or instinctive tendency which gives that idea driving force or energy. In crowd phenomena there are usually to be noted, as we have seen, fixation of attention and emotional excitement. The skilful orator knows how to play upon the emotions of his hearers. Once such emotions are aroused, all suggestions that harmonize with the system appealed to will be welcomed and others will be rejected, with the result that the usual control exercised by the critical faculties will be in abeyance. The particular emotional and instinctive tendencies involved will vary with the object which is the centre of attraction; but in all probability there is always in crowds present a sort of nervous exaltation produced by a heightening of the social instincts, a feeling of pleasurable excitement due to the knowledge that one is sharing ideas and emotion with a large number of people at the same time. This exaltation acts on leaders and people in different ways. The leader may become unusually aggressive and say things which he would not dream of saying under different circumstances; the people are readier to accept the suggestion of the leader. Further, in crowds the individual is, as Le Bon points out, apt to lose his sense of responsibility both because responsibility is divided and because his doings are masked by anonymity. Add to these factors the rapid repetition of stimuli and the volume of suggestion in big crowds and their low intellectual level becomes readily intelligible. Lack of responsibility and increase of suggestibility account also for the credulity of crowds. Their dogmatism and intolerance are due to the sense of omnipotence and the intensification of conviction characteristic of individuals in crowds.

The intensification or exaltation of the emotions is another much dwelt on aspect of crowds. In certain gregarious animals fear and anger spread like lightning. This is due no doubt to their conditions of life, their dependence on mutual aid, and the importance of prompt and united response to any signs of danger. In human crowds there is as we have seen a kind of vague exaltation akin to the gregarious instinct which makes the individual more responsive to stimuli. There is also the effect of the cumulative repetition of the stimulus.

Further, protected by anonymity, people do not exercise as much control as usual and give free zein to the expression of their feelings. Hence the shouting, gesticulating, boisterous laughter, frantic cheers of the crowd and their tendency to extremes. These exaggerated reactions cannot but have their effect on already suggestible individuals and so the process of cumulative suggestion goes on. The peculiar feeling of irresponsibility on the part of the individual is furthered by anonymity, but is very likely also due to the illusion of omnipotence felt by people sharing in a great assembly.

A great deal has been written about the immorality of crowds, but in this respect as in so many others much confusion has arisen from the use of collective terms. Crowds are in themselves neither good nor evil, but they may become either the one or the other on occasions according to the stimulus. Crowds may be brutal, but they may also be generous, sympathetic. An orator may appeal to the bad side as well as to the good side of human nature and the power of cumulative suggestion may act in either direction. Of course crowd action cannot in the nature of the case be based on rational deliberations, and its liability to suggestion makes it the victim of rapid alternation from one extreme to another. But there is no reason for saying that in a crowd individuals return to a primitive supposedly non-moral state.

We can now discuss some of the other explanations that have been put forward to account for the phenomena of crowd psychology. Many of them are based on the theory of Le Bon that in a crowd a new entity or mind comes into being differing in character from the minds of the individuals composing it. That is why, it is maintained, individuals in a crowd feel, think and act in a manner quite different from that in which each would feel, think, will and act were he in isolation. Of the existence of such new entities there is no direct evidence whatever. All that we are entitled to say is that when individuals are in a crowd, they are subject to certain influences which affect their emotions and thoughts. They are, for instance, more suggestible, less critical, less self-reliant, less responsible. The unanimity of crowds is greatly exaggerated. The suggestibility of individuals in crowds varies enormously, and there are some who retain their critical faculties and withstand the prestige of the herd. Further, the suggestibility, as one would expect, is limited by the character of the instincts and emotions aroused. If the suggestion is glaringly out of harmony with the emotional predisposition of the mob, it may be met with jeers. It seems an easy way out of a difficulty to postulate a new mind to which are ascribed all sorts of qualities – credulity, impulsiveness, irrationality, etc.

Another suggested explanation is also based on the theory of Le Bon and consists in the statement that in the crowd the unconscious qualities obtain the upper hand, i.e. there is reversion to the instincts or the substratum of the unconscious. Of this, as McDougall has shown, there is no evidence – except in a few cases, such as revivals. In any case to attribute to a permanent sub-conscious self all sorts of qualities of which there is no direct evidence is taking refuge in an asylum of ignorance. A third explanation also made familiar by Le Bon is that the crowd has a sort of magnetic influence inducing in those present a state resembling that of the somnambulist or hyponotized subject. This is certainly an exaggeration. There are certain resemblances between hypnotized subjects and mobs in action, but the differences are just as marked. In particular the somnambulist usually forgets what he did during his lapse, while members of a crowd remember. Further, the usual symptoms of hypnotism, changes in breathing, etc., are absent. All that is true in this theory is that individuals in a crowd are more suggestible. In truth, however, none of these explanations is needed. The fact that individuals in a crowd behave and think differently than when in isolation is simply a particular case of the responsiveness of individuals to environment. In the presence of others, there is a heightening of the social instincts, producing a vague exaltation which urges leaders to take the lead and to 'let themselves go' in doing so and others to follow the lead. This exaltation makes both more suggestible, the leader to the mood of the mob, and *vice versa*. The suggestibility varies according to the objects of attraction. In all, the knowledge that our ideas and feelings are shared by many is encouraging. Thus a process of cumulative suggestion goes on, which tends to inhibit conflicting ideas and emotions and to give to those in the focus dynamic force and energy. Accompanying this exaltation is a feeling of omnipotence and a consequent loss of the sense of personal responsibility. There is also to be noted a concentration of attention and a narrowing of consciousness which results in the absence of the usual controlling ideas and ideals. When to this is added the fact that the intellectual level of a crowd is generally low because only the qualities common to all are appealed to, it will be seen that all the phenomena usually noted in mobs and simple crowds can be accounted for.

CHAPTER X

The Public and Public Opinion

THE PUBLIC MAY be described as an unorganized and amorphous aggregation of individuals who are bound together by common opinions and desires, but are too numerous for each to maintain personal relations with the others. It differs from the crowd in the following points.

1. In the first place the public rests not on physical personal contact, but on communication by means of the Press, correspondence, etc. There is therefore absent the hurly-burly of the mob and consequently individuality can be retained more easily. There is also absent the heightening of the social feelings, which seem to be induced, at any rate to some extent, by bodily presence, and to this extent individuals in the public are less suggestible.

2. Secondly, while one can belong to one crowd only at a time one can and one often does belong to different publics at the same time. For instance, one may be a reader of several newspapers. Suggestions coming from different publics will tend to neutralize one another or to lead to a suspense of judgement and to further discussion.

3. Though through space-annihilating devices news can be rapidly communicated, there is not the same degree of simultaneity of stimulation that is present in crowds, and this lessens suggestibility.

4. Though the public is itself amorphous, it does generate organizations and these develop various devices against the mob mind such as rules of debate and the like.

These and similar distinctions between the crowd and the public have frequently been emphasized of late by critics of the 'psychology of the crowd', and it has been argued that because of these distinctions, individuals in the public are not so suggestible as members of a crowd. It should, however, be remembered that in some respects the force of suggestion of the public is infinitely greater than that of the crowd. In the first place, the public is in modern societies enormously large and complex, and its prestige is correspondingly greater than that of a mere crowd. Very few individuals can resist an opinion which is widely accepted and diffused and which comes with the authority of a vast public. In the second place, there exist in modern societies agencies for the deliberate formation or distortion of opinion, agencies which make use of a formidable machinery of cumulative suggestion, often more powerful and enduring in its effects than the repetition of the stimulus observable in crowds. These agencies deliberately and consciously practise the power of collective and repeated suggestion and use the crowd itself as a medium through the aid of the platform, the pulpit, the 'pictures', as well as and most of all, the Press. Mass suggestion is practised on the public on an enormous scale at all times, though perhaps this fact becomes more obvious in times of crisis, when powerful emotional and instinctive tendencies come into play, reduce the critical faculty of individuals, and lower them all to a common level in which all that is distinctive and personal is lost or submerged. Though therefore the mentality of the public is, at any rate in normal times, more rational and less explosive, it does have many elements in common with that of the crowd in the narrower sense of that term.

Modern society is especially characterized by the complexity of its publics, and a proper understanding of their relations to one another and to the institutions and associations to which they give rise is essential in order to get a real grasp of the nature of public opinion. We have seen that the conception of organism and mind alike exaggerate the unity of community. The latter consists of a series of groupings, partly coincident, partly divergent, and best represented as a series of circles some of which are concentric whilst others cut across each other. Individuals may and do belong to many of these circles or groupings and the closeness of their relations to them varies enormously. Moreover, the groupings themselves are not fixed, but are in a state of flux and subject to constant motion and transformation. Within each of the groupings there is a mass of operative ideas and sentiments, the result of a process of communication and reciprocal influence. Within each there grow up associations, i.e. organizations for securing common ends and institutions, i.e. definite or sanctioned or crystallized modes of relationship between the members of the group. The group, however, always retains within itself more than can be expressed in its associations and institutions. The relations that exist between the members of a social group are too rich and varied to be capable of embodiment in what are bound to be more or less mechanical modes of arrangements. Behind the organizations and institutions which are thus in a sense ways of action of the public there is always a mass of uncrystallized and 'floating' ideas whose influence is exhibited in the changes that occur in institutions and which occasionally receives direct expression in emergencies; for when the public cannot create an organization, it generates a crowd. Each group has its own mass of operative ideas, sentiments, desires. Since individuals belong to different circles at the same time there are naturally many common elements among the different publics. This circumstance, combined with the fact that the groupings are in constant movement, results in a steady clash and contact of ideas and the consequent overflow of ideas from one circle to another, at least in progressive and non-stratified societies. The public is thus an agglomeration or complex of publics, and when we say that an opinion is public we mean that among the several public opinions that exist within each of the groupings or minor publics, on the subject in question, this particular one predominates.

This predominance does not imply unanimity; certainly if unanimity is insisted upon, then the sphere of public opinion must be very restricted. This much, however, seems certain. We cannot speak of a public at all, at least in relation to government by public opinion, unless we refer to a body of individuals who are held together by the bond of common ideas and sentiments and who have at least a dim desire to maintain and continue their union. In groups in which there is a really deep cleavage there can be no public opinion. This becomes apparent in times of open and bitter class conflict. Appeals are then frequently made to public opinion and very often the fact is ignored that though those parts of the community against whom the appeal is made are themselves parts of the public in the wider sense, they yet for the time being, at any rate, constitute a public of their own, with interests of their own. The question of numbers is here not very relevant; for a minority cannot consider itself bound by the opinion of the majority, unless it recognizes a fundamental community of interests sufficient to override temporary differences. It follows that if the word public does not imply unanimity, mere acceptance by a majority is not sufficient to make an opinion public. It is necessary, as Lowell[1] points out, that there should be sufficient community of interest to make the minority feel itself bound to accept the opinion of the majority, and this implies a certain amount of homogeneity and the absence of 'irreconcilables'. To constitute an opinion public the following three conditions appear to be necessary. First, it must be widely held in a group that has a certain 'consciousness of kind', a feeling of ultimate identity of interests. Secondly, it must be a co-operative product, the result of the meetings of many minds in community. Thirdly, there must be a general recognition of its wide diffusion, a realization by each individual that it is the common opinon (Cf. Tarde's *Sense of Actuality*). By public opinion is thus meant the mass of ideas and judgements operative in a community which are more or less definitely formulated and have a certain stability and are felt by the people who entertain or hold them to be social in the sense that they are the result of many minds acting in common and more or less conscious that they are acting in common.

So far we have been dealing with the term 'public'. We now turn to the meaning of 'opinion'. Tarde would exclude desire and volition from the connotation of opinion, whilst others, as

[1] *Public Opinion and Popular Government.*

Lowell, slur over the distinction and tend to identify popular opinion with what is often called the general will. Those who have studied public opinion have chiefly devoted their attention to the sphere of politics and here, owing to the complexity of the problems, the confusion or identification of the two terms is easily made. Both conceptions are very vague and the line of demarcation is certainly difficult to draw. When we speak of government by public opinion we certainly do mean much the same as when we say government is an expression of the general will. It follows from our discussion of the general will, that the forces that govern social action are not, so far as they are the result of self-conscious voluntary acts, general, whilst those that are general cannot be said to be due to acts of will in the strict sense. What is really general in a community is a vague desire for the maintenance of the social structure, a sense perhaps of the congruity or incongruity of any new proposals with the habitual or customary ideas of a people; but these vague mental elements can hardly be spoken of as will. Now if we examine the subjects in regard to which public opinion in the sphere of government is influential, we shall find that they are confined to issues of a grave and vital character which call forth responses due to well-established traditions or other age-long forces, because they are vaguely felt to threaten the stability of the whole social structure; and these semi-instinctive reactions are also the core of what reality there is in the general will. Nevertheless, the sphere of public opinion is wider than that of the general will and perhaps greater validity attaches to the former conception. For will should, strictly speaking, be confined to the acts of a self-conscious personality, and whether even the gravest social decisions are the results of such conscious acts on the part of the general public may well be doubted. The term opinion, on the other hand, is much vaguer and may not inappropriately be used for that medley of latent prepossessions, established habits and customs, vague desires and confused ideas, which constitute the mental forces that are actually operative in society. It is worthy of note that some writers who have rejected the conception of a general will, alleged to be inerrant or always in the right, erect in its place the conception of popular opinion to which they ascribe a superiority to that of the average of individuals and even to the opinions which the best individuals could form for themselves. This is for example what is done by Dr McDougall.[1] He does not seem to realize that what he claims for popular opinion is exactly what Rousseau and Bosanquet claim for what they style the general will, and just as for McDougall popular opinion is best interpreted by the best minds of the community, so Rousseau needed a 'wise legislator' to determine what the popular will demands. The truth seems to be that the wisdom and inerrancy of popular opinion and general will alike are simply taken for granted in both cases without prior investigation into their real nature. As to the general will, investigation shows that what is general is not will and what is will is not general. The most we can say with regard to the community at large is that it either tacitly accepts the decisions of the few or is simply apathetic and indifferent or else shows more or less vague signs of discontent. Of course we may in a sense speak of a growing moral sense of the community, but it must be clearly understood that this would compare very unfavourably with the clear moral reflections of the best individuals and it certainly cannot be described as a moral will. So too with regard to the wider conception of opinion, we may say that it consists of the responses or reactions of the more passive members of a community to the stimulus of the more active. But these responses are of the most varied character. Public opinion, says Schmoller,[2] is like a harp of a million strings upon which there play winds from all directions. The sounds that emerge are not always unitary or harmonious. The most varied streams of melody cut through each other. It is subject to constant change both in regard to the objects on which it is directed and in regard to the mental elements through which it works. Now it demands this, now that. To-day it works on the passions; tomorrow it makes its appeal to calm deliberation. The word opinion is thus appropriately chosen; for in the history of

[1] *The Group Mind*, p. 192 f.

[2] *Grundriss*, I, p. 14.

thought opinion has always been contrasted with adequate knowledge and has been characterized by the fact that it is based on hearsay evidence, rough empirical generalizations on a mere enumerative basis, and accepted traditions and prepossessions. Opinion may thus be distinguished from reason or adequate knowledge, on the one hand, and from mere momentary impressions on the other. Whilst the former rests on scientific grounds and proceeds by the analysis of all the available evidence and the establishment of necessary connexions and relations, it seems clear that on the vast majority of subjects on which there is a considerable amount of relatively stable opinion, the people who hold those opinions have had no chance of weighing the evidence, nor are they competent to analyse or dissect the evidence with anything like the care and scrutiny that would be required for genuine scientific inference. The non-rational elements that enter even in the most important public decisions have been sufficiently emphasized of late and need not be further discussed here. On the other hand opinion is not the same thing as a momentary impression or instinctive response to a stimulus. It seems clear, for example, that the kind of response that is evoked in the mind of a person reading the words 'Hang the Kaiser' on a placard, does not deserve the name opinion, though no doubt much that enters into opinion owes its origin to a steady repetition of similar appeals to the instincts and emotions. Opinion, in other words, stands for that mass of ideas and beliefs in a group or society, which has a certain stability and is not a mere series of momentary reactions, but is yet not based on clearly thought out grounds of a scientific character. The meaning of the term public has been previously explained as referring to a group of people more or less amorphous, though it may contain some organizations and institutions within it. In each such group there will be a mass of ideas originally initiated by the more active members, but subsequently profoundly modified by contact with other ideas and frequently assuming a guise in the end which their originators would not acknowledge or recognize. Public opinion is thus a social product, due to the interaction of many minds. But it

should be noted that the ideas which emerge from the struggle
are not always the best logically speaking. Popular opinion is
subject to the most amazing vagaries. The ultimate reasons why
some ideas get stamped in and others stamped out are often
found in factors which are not under rational control, in complicated circumstances of the time, in an appeal to powerful
instinctive and emotional tendencies, but dimly or not at all
understood by the people whom they influence. There is, as has
frequently been pointed out, a sort of natural 'selection' of ideas,
but the 'fittest' are not always the best logically or ethically
speaking, but merely the most adapted to the particular circumstances. 'A change of belief arises in the main,' says Professor
Dicey, 'from the occurrence of circumstances which incline
the majority of the world to hear with favour theories which,
at one time, men of common sense derided as absurdities,
or distrusted as paradoxes' (*Law and Opinion in England*,
Lecture II).

He gives many striking illustrations. For example, between
1783–1861 the religious beliefs and political institutions of the
whole of the United States were, except as regards slavery,
the same; yet in the North slavery was condemned, whilst in
the South it was justified. The difference in attitude can only
be referred to a difference of circumstances. Again it is notorious
that while under the sway of powerful impulses and emotions
aroused in war-time people will readily accept ideas and believe
in them sincerely which they would be most sceptical of in
normal times. Even in normal times, popular thinking is swayed
by unconscious 'complexes' to a much greater extent than is
commonly realized.

We cannot thus find any evidence for the proverbial wisdom
and inerrancy of popular opinion, and it might even be maintained, with Hegel, that to be independent of it is the first
condition for anything that is great and rational. Nor does an
inductive inquiry into the manner in which public opinion operates lend support to such glorifications of it as are implied in
describing it as the 'social conscience' of the community,
'*vox dei*' and the like. The frown and favour alike of public

opinion are fretful and capricious and seldom betray discrimination or judgement. High on the crest of popular approval
the jockey, the boxer, the writer of society novels share their
honours with the philanthropist, the world-revolutionalizing
inventor, the great thinker. Public opinion reacts most quickly
and surely just in these cases, when the force of habit and
instinct is so strong, that the acts against which it exerts so much
violent pressure are in any case not likely to spread.[1] In times of
crisis, public opinion reveals clearly, more often than not, its
utter incapacity to serve as a moral will. Instinctive resentment
then takes the place of calm judgement. The unity which the
public exhibits in such times is due not to a genuine reconcilia-
tion of differences, but to a narrowing of consciousness with
consequent loss of intellectual control and the triumph of the
unitary or uniform modes of reaction due to biological and social
heredity. Discussions as to the value of public opinion have
always exhibited a remarkable tendency to emphasize extremes.
'Non est consilium in vulgo, non ratio, non discrimen non
intelligentia,' says Cicero, and Flaubert speaks of the people
as an 'immoral beast' or an eternal infant that will always be the
last in the hierarchy of the social elements. In recent times many
writers dismiss the opinion of the people as of no value on the
grounds of its instability and high suggestibility. On the other
hand, to public opinion has often been ascribed a sagacity and
trustworthiness greater than that which can be claimed for the
greatest individuals. On grave issues it is commonly alleged the
public verdict is always right and in matters of art and literature
it is 'time' that tells. Professor Bosanquet tells us frankly that 'in
public opinion we have an actual existent contradiction. As
public it is sound and true, and contains the ethical spirit of the
State. As expressed by individuals, in their particular judgements on which they plume themselves, it is full of falsehood
and vanity. It is the bad which is peculiar and which people
pride themselves on; the rational is universal in its nature
though not necessarily common'. In dealing with these contra-
dictory views, it should be remembered that to speak of the

[1] See Ross, *Social Control*, p. 98.

public as immoral and foolish is just as misleading and mischievous as to describe it as always in the right and as the highest
embodiment of spirit. Both descriptions alike imply an ascription to the general public of a fictitious unity and identity which
it does not possess. In the second place, to make any statements
about the wisdom and goodness, the folly and wickedness of
public opinion in general is utterly futile. We must take into
consideration the kind of public involved, the organization that
exists for collective deliberation and the sort of subjects in
regard to which a decision is required. The public opinion that
exists in a group of biologists with regard to the main principles
of the theory of evolution may be eminently enlightened, but
their opinion as to the right to strike on the part of the miners
may be decidedly prejudiced and uninstructed. In dealing with
the value of public opinion we have therefore to remember both
the complexity of the publics of modern societies and their
inter-relations and the complexity of the problems with which
they have to deal; and the consideration of these two points
would involve an analysis and classification of publics, an
exhaustive account of their specific problems and the means that
they possess for collective deliberation and intercommunication
with other publics. Meanwhile attention may be drawn to the
fact that the real value of public opinion in relation to government has lain not in the peculiar wisdom of its decisions, but
in quite other considerations. In the first place public opinion is
of importance not so much *qua* opinion, but *qua* public. Publicity is a *sine qua non* of sociality; and it has well been said that
the degree of publicity prevailing in a society is a direct measure
of the degree of its inner connectedness. Public approval and
disapproval is a tremendous force, and though not always enlightened it does nevertheless act as a check on the designs of
those who wield power in society. The value of public opinion
from this point of view lies not in its power of initiation but of
control. The blessings it thus confers are, it is true, not un-
mixed. History is full of the most poignant struggle of new ideas
against the apathy, indifference and sullen opposition of the
mass of mankind, but still the control cannot be dispensed with

and all efforts should be directed towards making it enlightened and open to reasoned persuasion.

In the second place, public opinion is of importance in relation to government for the simple reason that it is an existent fact of the greatest magnitude and that to defy it would certainly lead to disaster. Government must be by consent, and, as Aristotle pointed out long ago, to exclude any large number of people from a share in government is exceedingly dangerous, for this would mean the constant presence in the State of an element hostile to the Government and perpetually discontented. Of course, government by public opinion from this point of view does not in modern States involve a direct share on the part of each citizen in the actual deliberations of the Government, but merely a general agreement or consensus in regard to the legitimate character of the ruling authority, e.g. a general consent that the opinion of the majority shall prevail. It should be added that for government by public opinion, as Lowell points out, the opinion must be such that while the minority may not share it, they feel bound by conviction, not fear, to accept it, and if democracy is complete the submission of the minority must be given ungrudgingly. To what extent this latter condition is realized in modern communities is difficult to ascertain. For the majority of voters submission to government is based upon not much more than dumb acquiescence without exhibiting much of the element of free choice, whilst there are certainly growing up minorities who if they submit at all, do not do so ungrudgingly.

In the third place, we may refer to a point made by Aristotle in this connexion. He shows that although in regard to knowledge the ignorant many compare unfavourably with the expert few, yet often the best judge of a thing is not the expert who made it, but the people who have to use it. Thus the guest can often judge better of a feast than the cook, the master of a house better than the builder. So too it may be supposed the people who are ruled will know best where the governmental shoe pinches.

In the fourth place, perhaps the most important justification for government by public opinion lies in its educative value.

The public can only learn to think by thinking, just as it can only learn to govern itself by governing itself. This has always been the real defence of democratic rule and at present its significance is becoming more and more obvious. The abuses of government by public opinion are due to a large extent to the existence of agencies for deliberate distortion and to the fact that the majority of people are either not endowed with universal minds which would enable them to take an enlightened interest in large and difficult problems or else are so busy with their own affairs that they cannot find much opportunity for exhibiting their public spirit. The first of these causes of abuse can be met by the institution of a free and independent Press and by better education generally. The second raises more difficult problems of social organization and with it is connected a third cause of difficulty, viz. the enormous complexity of the problems with which a modern community has to deal. It is gradually coming to be recognized that for public opinion to be a really helpful force, there is need of much decentralization and division of power. In particular an arrangement of associations on a functional basis would simplify enormously the issues dealt with and would render possible the existence of an enlightened public opinion within each association, at any rate as regards its own specific problems. Great care, however, will have to be taken to prevent these associations from becoming self-centred and exclusive and to secure the means for the conduction of feeling and opinion from one group to another. In definitely stratified communities there is no easy intercommunication between the various groups. The result is stagnation and imperviousness to the demands of the general public on the part of each group. If a functional organization be adopted, therefore, it will be more than ever necessary to encourage free and fearless criticism, to perfect the means of intercommunication and above all, to prevent stratification by the institution of an organization which will include members from different functional organizations and represent those interests which they have in common. It will result from this that within each group or circle opinion would be instructed as far as its own affairs are concerned, and because of the presence in each group of members of the general organization there would be an overflow of ideas from one group to another and this would make possible the development of an enlightened public opinion on general matters too. To some extent this is the kind of organization that is contemplated by the Guild Socialists, but whether the latter theory be accepted or not, the need for division of functions with a view of diminishing the complexity and number of the problems that have to be dealt with, say by Parliament, is now generally admitted.

CHAPTER XI

The Psychology of Organization and Democracy

THE RELATIONS THAT exist between individuals in community are of an infinite variety and complexity. Many of them are so subtly and delicately interwoven that they escape formulation or organized sanction, but a large number depend for their permanent existence on explicit organization. The essence of organization is the co-ordination and adjustment of the activities of the individuals who have formed an association with a view to the attainment of a common end. Organizations can therefore only be understood by reference to the ends or purposes of the associations for which they exist and which they endeavour, consciously or unconsciously, to realize. It must be clearly understood that though associations rest on common interests, these interests are not always clearly apprehended by all their members, and are not pre-willed by them. Into some associations men are born; into others they are driven by mass suggestion or the prestige of an orator. Many of them exist for purposes which have never been clearly thought out by anyone, contain conflicting elements, and are rather of the nature of trial and error experiments than examples of conscious volition. Still more rudimentary associations rest on instinct, i.e. the mutual interdependence and co-operation of the members is achieved through the instrumentality of the social instincts. As intelligence develops the purposes of the associations become consciously realized and deliberately striven for. In all cases the mutual interdependence is due to the fact that all the parts are seeking to attain a common end, but, in the earlier phases, the end is not consciously apprehended and the actions of the members though purposive are not purposeful, while in the higher forms the ends or purposes come to be clearly apprehended by all or the majority of the members.

The instinctive basis persists even in advanced forms of associations, but it is profoundly transformed by the superstructure of experience and tradition. The instincts of taking the lead and following the lead, the gregarious instincts, the social impulses generally, are called into the service of social organization and form the nucleus of powerful sentiments having various social aggregates for their objects. By trial and error and later by conscious thought, definite modes of relationship between the members, securing division of labour and co-ordination, are established and come to have social prestige and authority. Thus there come to be the rules and institutions which express the formal relations of the individuals within the association, and embody the effort of the association to persist and maintain itself, and to secure the means for the harmonious co-operation of all the members. This effort towards harmony and unity is often, it must be admitted, feeble enough, and very often the means for its realization are found in the oppression of the spirit of individual aspiration of many of the members. In other words, the unity sought is one of subordination and elimination of differences rather than of an articulated system. Moreover, it is only in the latest phases of development that an attempt is made to think out the purposes for which social organization exists, and even then it is doubtful how much real and directive influence such conscious theorizing exerts, and whether in large and complex societies, at any rate, we have gone beyond the stage of trial and error.

All organizations that have any permanence, use, though in varying degrees, the processes of habituation and suggestion which are very potent instruments for securing collective action, if not collective volition proper. This fact is more obvious in organizations like armies, whose disciplinary drill is designed to inculcate the habit of immediate and unreflecting response to command and to heighten or enhance the responsiveness and suggestibility of each soldier to the influence of his superiors. But habit and suggestion are operative also in more complex societies, and to a much greater extent than is commonly realized. The whole system of education is designed to inculcate certain habits of feeling, thought and action. Tradition transmits the customs or habits of past generations and lends them an enormous prestige. In social organization habit is, therefore, a fundamental condition of the perpetuation of custom, and therefore a conservative force of great importance. It is in this connexion that the phrase 'social habits' is sometimes used. The reference is to modes of activity persistent in society which individuals come to perform automatically or with a minimum of consciousness, by dint of frequent repetition, originally at the instigation of others. Such social habits are of great importance as helping to conserve modes of behaviour which the experience of the race has shown to be useful and because, like all habits, they facilitate and simplify action, minimize fatigue and economize effort, and thus secure the release of our higher energies for higher processes demanding a great degree of attention. Habit is thus not necessarily the enemy of alertness and responsiveness, or rather theoretically it need not be so. In fact, however, it does often operate as the 'perambulator of human life', and helps to keep alive many institutions and modes of thought which have long since lost their real meaning and function.

The process of suggestion is also constantly and increasingly being used in the 'Great Society'. Advertising and propaganda generally deliberately make their appeal to powerful emotional tendencies and instincts, the arousal of which tends to inhibit conflicting ideas and therefore to reduce the powers of criticism to a low level. Further, by dint of steady repetition, they have an enormous cumulative effect, moulding the opinions and sentiments of their publics and, what is perhaps more dangerous, subtly creating in their victims the illusion that they are really thinking for themselves instead of receiving their opinions ready made. Another important factor in group-formation and in social organization generally is the development of sentiments

which have for their object or nucleus   oup
or society and also the group or society   ular
the sentiment summed up in the word   reat
importance. Long association and ca   ιe, the sharing of
common dangers and hardships, the development of a common
tradition and common modes of behaviour, all contribute to
make the association or group as such the centre of a large
number of emotional dispositions and the object of a sentiment
of loyalty, with the result that the individual members come to
think of the honour and dignity of the association with a certain
amount of emotional warmth and to identify themselves with it.
The history of the developments of this and similar sentiments
has not been studied in detail, so far as I know, but there can be
no doubt that they lie at the very root of group psychology.

The psychology of leadership and of the psychical relation
between leaders and led has also been much neglected, and is
only now beginning to receive the attention of scientific investigators. In particular, the whole question of the psychical basis of
authority will have to be studied in greater detail than has been
the practice. It is probable that the science of Psycho-analysis
will throw valuable light on this and kindred problems of social
psychology.

Sir Martin Conway, in a recent book, has given a helpful
classification of leaders. He distinguishes three types of leaders
whom he calls crowd compellers, crowd exponents and crowd
representatives. To the first belong people like Alexander and
Napoleon, men who can conceive a great idea, mould a crowd
big enough to carry it into effect and force the crowd to do it,
men who can stamp their individuality upon the people whom
they lead. The second class of leaders, the crowd exponents,
are men of peculiarly sympathetic insight and sensitiveness of
nature, and who are able to feel as the crowd feels or is going to
feel, to give clear and emphatic expression to that emotion, to
render articulate what is only vaguely and dimly felt or thought
by the mass. Sir Martin Conway quotes Bagehot's account of
Gladstone in illustration: 'No one half guides, half follows the
moods of his audience more quickly and more easily than Mr

Gladstone. There is a little playfulness in his manner which contrasts with the dryness of his favourite topics and the intense gravity of his earnest character. He receives his premises from his audience like a vapour and pours out his conclusions upon them like a flood. He will imbibe from one audience different vapour of premises from what which he will receive from another.' Sir Martin Conway himself instances Mr. Lloyd George. 'He is the visible and audible incarnation of popular tendencies. His emotions respond as sensitively to those of a crowd as ever a barometer to changes in atmospheric pressure. He has never manifested any trace of an individual mind or of an independent thought. He has added nothing to the stock of political ideas, but has perfectly voiced the ideas of the crowd by which he acts and from which he draws his emotions and his power' (*The Crowd in Peace and War*, p. 107).

To the third category belong the crowd-representatives, who only express known and settled opinion of the crowd, and who, like constitutional monarchs, are hedged round with conditions which prevent them from giving utterance to their own independent views, if any such they have. There exists a vast literature dealing with the machinery of leadership, with the working of constitutions, of Parliament, of the party system, of the Press and the like. But it cannot be said that these subjects have been studied at all scientifically from the point of view of psychology, except perhaps by Professor Graham Wallas. It is safe to say that the best accounts have so far been written not by the professional psychologists, but by trained observers of human life who have come to study the subject from the point of view of other fields of human inquiry. There is now a very widely prevalent feeling of disillusionment in regard to the success of democratic institutions, and the points of weakness which have been revealed in them are essentially psychological in character. They may be grouped under the following heads.

1. The tendency inherent in all organization towards oligarchy.

2. The psychological difficulties in securing an adequate system of representation for complex interests.

3. The failure of the representative system, owing to the ignorance and gullibility of the masses, and the existence of agencies for the distortion of opinion.

4. The psychological difficulties in securing effective collective deliberation in large assemblies.

1. There are, of course, good technical and psychological reasons for the development of systems of representation.[1] The history of associations, whether of Trade Unions, political parties or States, shows that direct government is impossible on any large scale. Large masses of men cannot take counsel effectively even when simple issues are at stake, and with the growing complexity of affairs and the importance of rapid decisions they become unwieldy and ineffective. Further, direct government is liable to great abuse. Big assemblies are notoriously suggestible and fall a ready prey to the demagogue and orator, to the unscrupulous and ambitious. Again, even where direct government exists some authority is needed to deal with affairs that arise in the intervals between assemblies, and experience shows that the real power will soon come to be exercised by the officials charged with this function. Added to the technical difficulties of direct government are certain psychological factors working in the direction of leadership and representation. The forces that drive a structureless mass to seek some form of organization are not all conscious and deliberate, but have deeper roots in instinct and the unconscious. The majority of people seem to long to be led and are only too eager to obey authority, as is evidenced by the widespread cult of leaders and the universal readiness to submit to authority. Thus we find that in all societies of any permanence leaders emerge and achieve power. Now, in all organizations, whether they rest on hereditary leadership or leadership on a representative basis, there are strong tendencies towards oligarchy, due both to the technical nature of government with which we are not here concerned, and to certain psychological factors. The latter may be summed up under three heads: (a) the indifference and apathy of the masses and their longing for leadership; (b) the

[1] On this section cf. R. Michels, *Les Partis politiques*.

thirst for power on the part of the leaders; (c) the psychical metamorphosis of even the best leaders and their estrangement from the masses.

The laziness, indifference, and apathy of the masses is probably the obverse side, so to speak, of their longing for leadership. Possibly it is due to some extent to lack of imagination and the difficulty of understanding the complex problem confronting the citizen today. But it cannot be altogether due to these circumstances, for apathy is to be observed even in the majority of members of relatively small societies dealing with matters within the reach of ordinary intelligence. The result is that the masses exercise but an imperfect control over their leaders. Thus the conditions are given which are likely to corrupt even the most public spirited of leaders. For the latter must very speedily realize that though in theory they are supposed to represent and express the opinions and desires of their electors, the latter have, in fact, no opinions and no will of their own worth considering. In complex societies in particular, where the members vary greatly in education and intellectual equipment, the leader cannot be a mere exponent, but must be a moulder of opinion. Under favourable conditions, and given the existence of an alert and critical electorate, these circumstances would be conducive to genuine co-operative thinking, but, in the majority of cases, it merely leads to a gradual but constantly increasing estrangement of the leaders or representatives from the people whom they are supposed to represent and to a desire on their part to dominate the masses and use them as tools for the realization of their own ideas and schemes. In all parties the majority of the members are apathetic creatures of habit and suggestion, easily swayed by the power of the orator and that species of flatterers, the demagogue. One of the most marked characteristics of democratic organizations is their suggestibility to the magic of words, as is clearly seen from the great role that is played by orators and journalists. Often the qualification for leadership is not the power of clear, logical thought or exposition, but rather a certain versatility and power to jump from one subject to another, a facile and direct manner of speech, a skill in repartee; and men possessed of such powers are often opportunitists and readily become the tool of powerful interests.

The apathy of the masses and their longing for leadership is accompanied by an insatiable thirst for power on the part of the leaders. The desire to dominate is a deep rooted and powerful passion in some people. What is perhaps more important is that the possession of power leads to a profound change in the mentality of the leader. Bakunin urged that the possession of power will turn even the greatest lover of liberty into a tyrant. This statement has often been confirmed by facts. At first the leader may be convinced of the value of the principles for which he stands. Indeed, he may have been driven to assume the leadership by profound conviction of the importance of these principles and by a genuine belief in the possibility of his making a genuine contribution to their realization. But the taste of power is intoxicating. It creates the illusion of greatness and indispensableness and the consequent disinclination to abandon power once enjoyed. It is to be noted that the ambition for power often reveals the greatest intensity in the case of leaders of working-class origin. They are often capricious and despotic, and exhibit all the characteristics of the parvenu. The self-made man is often vain and liable to be moved by flattery. In the history of Socialism in all countries we meet with men characterized by the arrogance of the half-educated and the inverted snobbery of the upstart, and Socialist Parliamentary Parties often contain men of working-class origin who unconsciously yield to the powerful influence of the 'bourgeois' atmosphere, and end by going over to 'the enemy'. It is even arguable that leaders who genuinely believe themselves to be truly representative are more liable to become tyrannical than others. For they are likely to have a fanatical zeal to put things right and a passion for energetic government not so marked in others.

The incompetence of the masses, their apathy and indifference, their longing for leadership and worship of authority, together with the desire for power and domination on the part of the leaders, are thus factors working for oligarchy in all democratic communities. The question may be raised whether this tendency is essentially involved in democracy, or is due merely to the fact that, at present, Government and elections are so largely controlled by powerful economic interests. Michels has shown that the same factors are operative in all Socialist parties and maintains that organization as such implies oligarchy. The Syndicalists and Marxians, on the other hand, seem to think that genuine self-government will be possible after the 'revolution'. It is difficult to see any real justification for this belief. Any centralized form of government is bound to be oligarchical in tendency. 'Qui dit pouvoir dit domination et toute domination presume l'existence d'une masse dominée.' We are told that the State will wither away. But what will take its place? Surely there will either be a huge bureaucracy or some form of representation. But in that case there is certain to arise a new dominant minority. Is it not likely that the social revolution will but replace the existing dominant class by a clandestine oligarchy of demagogues working under the guise of equality? Again it is agreed that there must be an intermediate stage of dictatorship by a minority. Will that minority be willing to give up its power, once it has secured full control? It is probable also that the psychological changes mentioned above will also take place in the mentality of the dictators. This appears to be confirmed by the example of the Russian Revolution. 'It is sheer nonsense to pretend that the rulers of a great empire such as Soviet Russia, when they have become accustomed to power, retain the proletarian psychology and feel that their class interest is the same as that of the ordinary working man. This is not the case in Russia now, however the truth may be concealed by fine phrases. The Government has a class consciousness and a class interest quite distinct from the proletarian, who is not to be confounded with the paper proletarian of the Marxian scheme' (B. Russell, *Theory and Practice of Bolshevism*, p. 155).

2. The second line of criticism is associated with the theory of functional representation, particularly as worked out by Mr G. D. H. Cole. According to that theory, it is impossible for any one individual to represent or to act as a substitute for the whole will and personality of other individuals, though *it is*

possible and indeed desirable to have representatives for specific purposes. The individual is a centre of consciousness and will which are not as such communicable and transferable and is possessed of a power of self-determination which he never abandons. In associations aiming at a specific object representation does not imply any violation of the individuality of its members, but a system of representative government, based on the idea that individuals can be represented as wholes, is not only destructive of personal well-being but is practically impossible. 'In proportion as the purposes for which the representative is chosen lose clarity and definiteness, representation passes into misrepresentation and the representative character of the acts resulting from association disappears. Thus misrepresentation is seen at its worst today in that professedly omnicompetent "representative" body – Parliament – and in the Cabinet which is supposed to depend on it. Parliament professes to represent all citizens in all things, and therefore, as a rule, represents none of them in anything. It is chosen to deal with anything that may turn up quite irrespective of the fact that the different things that do turn up require different types of persons to deal with them. It is therefore peculiarly subject to corrupt, and especially to plutocratic, influences and does everything badly because it is not chosen to do anything well' (*Social Theory*, p. 108).

3. The complexity of the issues which have to be dealt within such a body as Parliament is responsible not only for the 'misrepresentation' of their electors by members once they are chosen, but also to some extent for the strange aberrations of elections. Owing largely to that complexity motives get so mixed and interests so confused that real representation becomes impossible and the persons elected owe their success largely to some one or more dominant issues which have the power of emotional and instinctive appeal. To speak of the representative as expressing a *common* will is clearly unjustifiable in the majority of the cases, for the motives that inspire the electors are very mixed and divergent and even conflicting. Add to these difficulties the political ignorance of the masses and

their gullibility and the existence of a highly developed machinery for steady and cumulative suggestion and the vagaries of elections become intelligible. 'In Great Britain,' says Mr H. G. Wells, 'we do not have elections any more; we have rejections. What really happens at a general election is that the party organization – obscure and secretive conclaves with entirely mysterious funds – appoint about twelve hundred men to be our rulers, and all that we, we so-called self-governing people are permitted to do is, in a muddled angry way, to strike off the names of about half these selected gentlemen.'[1]

4. Finally, there are psychological difficulties in the working of large assemblies which make real or effective collective deliberation impossible, with the result that real power comes to be concentrated in the hands of a very few people even in the most democratic Governments. It is interesting in this connexion to compare Dr McDougall's panegyrics of the British Parliament with the opinions of close observers of political life like Professor Graham Wallas or Ostrogorsky, or H. G. Wells. Dr McDougall regards parliamentary procedure as exemplifying genuine collective deliberation and volition. The representatives consist of men 'among whom custom and tradition accord precedence to the natural leaders, the most able, and those in whose consciousness the nation in the past, present and future is most adequately reflected'. Further, the party system and the Press ensure 'vigorous criticism and full discussion of all proposals under a system of traditional conventions evolved for the regulation of such discussions' (*The Group Mind*, p. 190). One wonders whether this opinion is warranted by psychological observation or is based on general political assumptions and predilections. With it may be contrasted the verdict of Professor Graham Wallas and other observers both in England and abroad who are impressed with the utter futility of the ostensible proceedings of Parliament, the intellectual slackness that prevails and the absence of any really organized discussion. Of course if national deliberation and national volition means the deliberation and volition of people in whom the 'idea of the

[1] Quoted, Lippmann, *Preface to Politics*, p. 291.

nation' is best reflected and if the 'best' people themselves decide that they best reflect the idea of the nation then Dr McDougall is undoubtedly right. But the 'idea of the nation' is too vague a phrase, and the national good often means in practice the good of the 'best' section of the nation. The outside observer cannot but be struck with the frequent absence of real integration of thought and of responsiveness to enlightened and instructed criticism that characterizes parliamentary debates. This absence of real collective volition is due, however, not merely to the triumph of sectional interests and conscious perversion of the popular will in so far as ascertainable, but to the actual psychological difficulties of collective deliberation in large assemblies dealing with subjects of constantly increasing complexity. It is in the latter respect in particular that the psychologist may be able to be of assistance. Generally the conclusion that emerges from the above discussion is that any policy of reconstruction that is to be of real value must aim at decentralization and division of labour, with a view of making the issues dealt with in any assembly more definite and less complex and more amenable to the system of representation, and, above all, it must be designed to secure a nation better educated, less apathetic, less suggestible, less amenable to externally imposed authority, more capable of independent and fearless thought, and of being stimulated by wider interests.

Conclusion

IT MAY BE well, in conclusion, to emphasize some of the main points of our discussion. In the first place, we argued that society or community was to be conceived as a network of individuals related to one another in an infinite number of ways and forming unities or wholes varying enormously in character and complexity. Some of the relations subsisting between individuals are susceptible of organization, and thus form the basis of associations and institutions, others are too subtle, personal and delicate and escape organization, others again are too vague to be formulated but are partly expressed in popular movements or tendencies, in public opinion and the like. These relations can only be understood in terms of mind, i.e. they rest upon impulses, ideas and purposes. But the whole that is formed by the members in relation is not correctly or usefully conceived as an organism or mind analogous to the organism or mind of an individual. The relations between individuals in society are indeed close and intimate. Sociality and individuality are, as Professor MacIver has recently urged with great emphasis, but two aspects of the same process, the development of personality. Nevertheless the individual is a unique focus or centre of reference, conscious of himself as a single whole, related in very different ways to the different social wholes of which he is a member, and his nature is not exhausted in his membership of those wholes. These again, it is true, form some sort of system, or rather we may discover in them a *nisus* or effort towards system. But, in the first place, the degree of unity actually attained by them must not be exaggerated, and, in the second place, in so far as there is real unity, it is a unity of purposes, of ideas and ideals, of spiritual content, and it has not the unity of process and substantive continuity characteristic of the individual mind.

We noted, in the second place, a very widely prevalent reaction against reason and even a sort of cult of the irrational. Now to a large extent this anti-intellectualist movement is due to an abstract view of reason which identifies it with a bare and cold logical faculty of comparing and relating and to a false separation between reason or rational will and impulse. It should, however, be remembered that the strength of the anti-intellectualist movement lies in the fact that it has emphasized points that were often ignored by the rationalists and that the latter are often guilty of the very same abstractions as those of the anti-intellectualists. The point of view we have sought to maintain is that social institutions do contain rational and purposive elements. They are experiments at a unitary life, and represent the more or less enlightened and co-ordinated efforts of mankind to discover the conditions of harmonious development. But for the most part they have hardly gone beyond the stage of trial and error and they certainly are not based upon clearly thought out schemes of life embodying organized systems of purposes. This, however, does not mean that the role of reason is unimportant. On the contrary, if by reason we understand a principle working within and by means of the impulses, and giving them unity of aim and direction, then reason is the very life of the whole social process. At any rate it follows from our account that what we want is not blind reliance upon mystical impulses, not less reason but more reason, more understanding, that is to say, of the conditions under which the impulses may be made to work together, so as to lead to the harmonious development of personality in society.

Bibliography

INTRODUCTION

Davis, M. M., *Psychological Interpretations of Society*.
McDougall, W., *Introduction to Social Psychology*.
Sganzini, Carlo, *Die Vortschritte der Völkerpsychologie Von Lazarus bis Wundt*.
Hurwicz, Elias, *Die Seelen der Völker*.
Ellwood, *Introduction to Social Psychology*

CHAPTER I

Hobhouse, L. T., *Mind in Evolution*.
McDougall, W., *Introduction to Social Psychology*.
Shand, A. F., *Foundations of Character*.
'Symposium on Instinct and Emotion', *Proceedings of the Aristotelian Society*, 1914–15.
Lloyd Morgan, C., *Instinct and Experience*.
Woodworth, R. S., *Dynamic Psychology*.

CHAPTER II

McDougall, W., *Introduction to Social Psychology*.
Trotter, W., *Instincts of the Herd in Peace and War*.
Bagehot, *Physics and Politics*.
Davis, M. M., *Psychological Interpretations of Society*.
Tarde, *The Laws of Imitation*.
Tarde, *Social Laws*.
Ross, *Social Psychology*.
Ellwood, *Introduction to Social Psychology*.
Hart, B., 'The Methods of Psycho-Therapy', *Proc. of the Royal Society of Medicine*, Vol. XII, 1918.

Prideaux, E., 'Suggestion and Suggestibility', *Journal of the British Psychological Society*, March, 1920.

CHAPTER III

Hobhouse, L. T., *Mind in Evolution.*
Hobhouse, L. T., *Development and Purpose.*
Stout, G. F., *Manual of Psychology.*
Hetherington and Muirhead, *Social Purpose.*

CHAPTERS IV AND V

McDougall, W., *The Group Mind.*
Bosanquet, B., *The Philosophical Theory of the State.*
Hobhouse, L. T., *The Metaphysical Theory of the State.*
Durkheim, E., *Les formes élementaires de la vie religieuse.*
Durkheim, E., 'Representations individuelles et representations collectives.' *Revue de Métaphysique et de Morale*, VI, 1898.
Gehlke, E., *E. Durkheim's Contribution to Sociological Theory.*

CHAPTER VI

Herbert, S., *Nationality and its Problems.*
Steinmetz, R., 'Der erbliche Rassen- und Volkscharakter', *Vierteljhrschrift fuer Wissensch., Philosophie und Soziologie*, 1902.
Fouillée, *Esquisse psychologique des peuples européens.*

CHAPTER VII

Wundt, E., *Facts of the Moral Life.*
Ross, E. A., *Social Control.*
Vinogradoff, Prof. P., *Common Sense in Law.*
Korkunov, *Theory of Law.*
Westermarck, E., *Origin and Development of Moral Ideas.*

CHAPTER VIII

MacIver, R. M., *Community.*
Cole, G. D. H., *Social Theory.*

Hetherington and Muirhead, *Social Purpose.*
Hobhouse, L. T., *Metaphysical Theory of the State.*
Russell, B., *Principles of Social Reconstruction.*

CHAPTER IX

Conway, Sir Martin, *The Crowd in Peace and War.*
Le Bon, *The Crowd.*
Graham Wallas, *The Great Society.*
Ross, E. A., *Social Psychology.*

CHAPTER X

Ross, E. A., *Social Psychology.*
Ross, E. A., *Social Control.*
Lowell, A. L., *Public Opinion and Popular Government.*
Dicey, A. V., *Law and Opinion in England.*
Sheppard, W. J., *American Journal of Sociology*, Vol. XV.

CHAPTER XI

Michels, *Political Parties.*
Cole, G. D. H., *Social Theory.*
Lippmann, W., *Preface to Politics.*

APPENDIX I

Psycho-analysis and Sociology

PSYCHO-ANALYSIS GREW up as a method for dealing with mental diseases, but the theories and principles which the experience thus gained suggested proved capable of much wider application. Freud himself in his various metapsychological writings used his analysis of the structure of personality and especially his classification of human instincts to throw light upon the nature of human groups, the foundations of morals and religion, and indeed of all the elements of culture. In this he has been followed by many of his disciples, and now there is hardly a branch of sociological inquiry which has remained unaffected by Freud's teaching of the part played by unconscious factors in the growth of the mind. The claims made are so far-reaching that it is the plain duty of sociologists to come to terms with them. The task presents great difficulties. Psycho-analysts claim that only those who have undergone analysis can properly appreciate the real significance of their theories. They have, moreover, evolved a highly technical and complicated terminology, which even if necessary for their proper purpose, often results in giving their ideas an air of novelty and even of mystery, which makes it very difficult to compare their views of social relations with those held by other sociologists. Furthermore, the field of inquiry is very wide and a full investigation would require a lengthy treatise. What I propose to do here is to examine briefly Freud's own sociological theories and to comment on some aspects of the present relations between psychopathology and sociology.

I

We may begin with Freud's theory of group psychology. In the course of an examination of the views of Le Bon, McDougall and Trotter, he argues, tentatively at first but with increasing assurance, that the tie that binds people together in a group is libidinal in character, or in other words, that social behaviour and sexual behaviour spring ultimately from the same source of energy, namely, the energy derived from the love instincts. The theory is linked by Freud with the hypothesis of the primal horde as the origin of society. In this the father is supposed to have exclusive possession of all the women. He has therefore to compel his sons to renounce their sexual desires. This renunciation constitutes a common bond between them and gives them the character of a group. In *Group Psychology* it is suggested that this hypothesis may be of the nature of a 'just so' story intended to illustrate in a vivid way the relations between the leader of a group and the members. It seems, however, from Freud's remarks in one of his latest writings (*Moses and Monotheism*) that it is to be taken as a serious reconstruction of the origins of society. In essentials, as it seems to me, Freud's views of the nature of human groups is independent of this hypothesis, and as I find no support for it in anthropological fact I propose to disregard it. As a first approximation Freud's view seems to amount to this. The bond that holds people together in a group is ultimately, that is to say in its unconscious roots, erotic in character. The sexual impulses have for various reasons to be repressed. This repression is made possible by the acceptance of standards or ideals of conduct that individuals can accept as their own, or in analytic terminology, make part of their ego-ideal. Now the growth of the ego-ideal depends upon the development of an attachment to a leader in whom the individual sees his ideal of himself. This tie with the leader constitutes a common quality shared by all the members of the group and leads them to identify themselves each with the others. Hence Freud defines the primary group as 'a number of individuals who have substituted one and the same object for their ego and have consequently identified themselves with one another in their ego' (*Group Psychology*, p. 80). If I have understood Freud aright, the statement that the social tie is libidinal in character means that the group depends for its cohesion on repressed or aim-inhibited sexuality made possible by the growth of a common tender tie with the leader. The examples that Freud gives are taken from associational groups such as armies and churches. Presumably in an inclusive community which contains more than associations the explanation would be fundamentally similar. In other words, the community consists of a complex hierarchy of libidinal structures held together by a common attachment to the ideals, or in Freudian language, 'the substitution of the same object for the ego ideals of the members'. On this interpretation the group structure is sexual in the sense that it rests on repression of sex impulses made possible by identification resting on a common tender tie with the leader or leader substitute. It will be noted that on this view the libidinal tie between the members of a group does not mean that they have a natural or direct 'love' for one another. On the contrary, the original feeling both in the nursery and the wider social group is one of mutual hostility. Freud quotes in this connexion Schopenhauer's famous simile of the freezing porcupines which crowd together to save themselves from being frozen to death, but separate again as soon as they feel one another's quills, until at length they discover a mean distance at which they can tolerably exist. Social feeling is thus not primary but involves, as Freud says, a reversal of an originally hostile feeling. This reversal comes about when the members recognize that they cannot each have the exclusive love of the leader, and in their common renunciation identify themselves with one another. Herein Freud finds the root of the sense of social justice. 'Social justice,' he says, means 'that we deny ourselves many things so that others may have to do without them as well, or what is the same thing, may not be able to ask for them.' The sense of a common interest, the building up of an *esprit de corps* and the like are thus ultimately rooted in a common jealousy. The demand for equality means that no one must want to put himself forward, that everyone must be the same and have the same.

There is, however, another side to Freud's teaching which, if fully developed, would result in a very different view of social relationships. This is connected with the very wide sense he gives to the term 'libido' in his later writings. In *Beyond the Pleasure Principle* he identifies the libido with the life instincts. It is, he says, 'the Eros that endeavours to impel the separate particles of living matter to one another and to hold them together'. In this sense it can be used to cover all forms of attraction, including even the attraction of cells within an organism. In this work and in *Das Unbehagen in der Kultur* it is given a metaphysial status as a force making for ever-widening synthesis and unity and which would, if left to itself, extend to the whole of humanity. Why this must happen we know not: '*das sei eben das Werk des Eros*'. On this view libido is not identical with sex. The sexual impulses are only a part of the libido, that namely which, as he says, 'is turned towards the object' (p. 79). If this be so, the interest that human beings have in each other, the need that they have for one another is not sexual in the narrow sense of the word, but may well be a primary form of libidinal attachment, and the theory of the social bond as resting on a diffused and aim-inhibited sexuality becomes unnecessary. It seems to me that there is here a real ambiguity in Freud's teaching. On the one hand, he wants to maintain that all forms of love, including not only sexual love but the love of self, the love of parents and children and devotion to abstract ideals are rooted in the sex impulses diverted from their original aim. On the other hand, the sexual impulses appear as only one species of a wide group of libidinal attachments with some of which they may indeed come into conflict. If a choice is to be made between these two views the latter seems to me clearly the more reasonable, especially if the notion of love or Eros is shorn of the mystical powers which Freud tends to ascribe to it in his more metaphysical moods. The social impulses could then be regarded as existing, so to speak, in their own right and not as derived from sex in the narrow sense by a process of transformation or redirection.

If this wider use of the notion of the libido be accepted, Freud's account of the sense of justice would have to be seriously revised. Freud offers no evidence for his view that the sense of justice is always rooted in envy and jealousy. No doubt in many cases the demand for equality may express a desire that other people shall be given no greater share than ourselves. No doubt again in some cases we are the more ready to relieve the suffering of another because to do so exalts our own ego. But what reason is there for doubting the existence of disinterested sympathy which is by all accounts one root of justice, or of the social feeling which is the emotional accompaniment of the slowly emerging demand for a rational ordering of social life, which gives the sense of justice its impetus? Is not, in short, the demand for justice in many cases the expression of a deeply felt desire for a rational order? Here as elsewhere in psycho-analytic writings the possibility of the existence of what may be called rational feeling is not explored.

II

The ambiguity of the notion of the libido affects very deeply Freud's theory of culture, worked out in another of his 'metapsychological' writings – *Das Unbehagen in der Kultur*[1] – to which I now turn. The theory is based on the distinction between two groups of instincts, the love instincts making for life and the aggressive or destructive instincts making for death. In the history of culture, as in life generally, Eros is pitted against Thanatos, and the struggle between them is the essential fact of human history. We have here in a new form the old theory of love and hate as primary forces.

The term 'culture' is used by Freud in a very wide sense to cover all the achievements which differentiate man from his animal ancestors. Broadly it includes all the activities which enable man to control natural forces in the service of human ends, the institutions regulating the relations between men, the

---

[1] English translation, *Civilization and its Discontents*.

achievements concerned with the search for beauty, cleanliness and order, the understanding and aesthetic appreciation of the world, including science, art, religion and philosophy. The process of culture consists in the transformation and redirection of the fundamental human instincts. This is effected in part by normal development, as when the interest in excecretions passes into the desire for order and cleanliness. In part the process is one of sublimation, that is, the redirection of libidinal energy which, Freud thinks, supplies the drive for the higher mental activities. In both these cases culture results in a fulfilment, direct or indirect, of fundamental drives. In other cases, however, culture involves not fulfilment but renunciation or repression of instincts. Herein Freud finds the deeper causes of the malaise of culture and this seems also the root of the pessimism which tinges Freud's whole discussion of human affairs; for repression or renunciation is essential to culture, yet cannot achieve liberation or harmony. In essentials the growth of culture means the growth of man's power over nature and the extension of social organization, that is the widening of the social group and the improvement of the mechanisms for regulating social relations. The group, according to Freud, begins with the family, based on genital love and the love of the mother for her children. The extension of the group is due to the operation of the libido in its aim-inhibited form and, left to itself, Eros would find expression in ever-widening units, culminating in the unity of the whole of mankind. Indeed, as we have seen, Eros almost comes to have metaphysical status analogous to the vital impulse of the philosophers and the principle of love in some of the religions. What, then, stands in his way and why in particular has it to be repressed? The answer seems to be two-fold. A fissure arises between the love demands of the family and the needs of the wider community. The community needs libidinal energy for its own purposes. Hence in part the restraints everywhere imposed on sex, restraints and inhibitions which, if they are to succeed, must begin in childhood. But, secondly, a deeper explanation is to be found in the existence of the death or aggressive instincts, which Freud regards as primary and ineradicable and which, uncontrolled, would shatter society. To control aggression aim-inhibited libidinal energy has to be used. The process involves the building up of the super-ego with the aid of which aggression is turned inwards and thus prevented from expressing itself directly. Nevertheless, the aggressive impulses are not eradicated. Every time we refrain from aggression our introverted aggression is strengthened and there is tension between the super-ego and the ego. The tension is felt as the sense of guilt. This is the price that men have to pay for culture. The repression which it involves demands compensation. Hence the need for substitute gratifications partly supplied by art. Hence also the building up of 'illusions' like religion, which offer man the promise of salvation and console him for the inevitable renunciations inherent in culture. It will be seen that Freud agrees with the teaching of the spiritual religions in laying emphasis on the great ethical importance of the principle of love. Unlike them, however, he can have no assurance of the ultimate triumph of love or its power to hold in check the aggressive impulses which, it seems, must forever threaten civilization.

Freud's essay on culture has a sombre grandeur of which my brief summary can have given no impression. Perhaps it belongs to the world of poetry at least as much as to the world of science. I want to consider it simply from the point of view of its inner coherence and its power to explain the course of culture. It seems to me that the ambiguity of the notion of the libido here occasions greater difficulty than even in the theory discussed above of the nature of social groups. For if by love is meant sex love in the narrower sense of the word, it is difficult to see how its control would necessarily liberate energy for social purposes. I do not know of any historical evidence tending to show that societies which exercise a rigid control over sexual relations are more productive in art or science or are less aggressive within and without than societies which allow greater sexual freedom. Freud certainly provides no such evidence. The attempt made by Dr J. D. Unwin[1] to show that in primitive societies there is a

[1] *Sex and Culture*, 1934.

definite relation between degree of sexual continence and degree of cultural change fails, I think, to carry conviction, his criteria for both cultural condition and sexual regulation being very vague. Purely theoretical argument in a matter of this sort must be very unreliable. For even if sexual restraint be regarded as resulting in the liberation of energy, it does not follow that this energy would necessarily be used for socially valuable purposes and not be put at the service of aggression or domination. Of the libido in the sense of sexual attachment it is surely too much to claim, as Freud does, that it alone is the civilizing agent or that it alone brings about a change from egoism to altruism (*Group Psychology*, p. 57). If love is needed to control hate we must admit the possibility of a love for others which is not identical with aim-inhibited sex love but underived and direct. From this point of view again it is more reasonable to accept the wider view of the libido as a genus including many species, qualitatively different, of which the many varieties of sex love, maternal love and family affections are the most obvious examples, but which is potentially of wider range and is, perhaps, as Freud says, capable of being extended to the whole of mankind.

Whether there is, as Freud holds, an independent impulse to destroy is a matter on which analysts are not agreed.[1] I am not convinced that there is in man a primary need to destroy or hurt as there is a need to love or to eat and drink. Aggressive behaviour is in most cases a response to interference with or thwarting of other dispositions, and, in other cases, a result of intensified self-assertion, which may begin in overcoming resistance and end in seeking resistance to overcome. Since in all societies there is plenty of thwarting and repression there is also bound to be plenty of aggression and consequently repression of aggression. Nevertheless it is not so much, or at least not only, the repression of aggression as the frustration and thwarting of other dispositions that is the cause of further aggression. This at any rate in its application to group relations is in harmony with the generalization suggested by Herbert Spencer that it is

---

[1] cf. Dr E. Jones, 'Psycho-analysis and the Instincts', *British Journal of Psychology*, Jan. 1936.

societies which are authoritarian within that are also militaristic without, while it is far from being established that it is the societies which encourage tolerance and peacefulness within that are the most prone to war. To the role of introverted aggression in the development of morality I shall return later. Meanwhile the effect of my argument so far is that the important element in Freud's theory is the insistence on repression as a source of frustration within and conflict without and on the subtle intermingling of love and hate in human relations. Both terms in this antithesis, however, stand in need of further clarification before they can be used as primary forces in explaining social life and cultural development.

It is, I think, remarkable that Freud has not made greater use in his general theory of culture of the contrast he draws between the ego and the id. These have a better claim to figure as the *dramatis personae* of history than Eros and Thanatos. The id consists according to him of the crude instinctual needs, the untamed passions, while the ego stands for the element of reason and circumspection and among its other functions is that of introducing unity and harmony between the warring impulses. But this unity cannot be achieved by love alone; for love can be as blind as hate. To control them both it is necessary to use intelligence and reason, to extend, in Freudian language, the organization of the id, by strengthening the ego and making it more and more independent of the unconscious elements of the mind.[1] Can we not see in history the groping effort of the human reason to achieve this control over unreason in individuals and groups, a problem growing in complexity as the scale of operation expands and the opportunities for union and discord alike multiply? This at any rate is the interpretation which Freud's survey suggests. The function of psycho-analysis, Freud tells us, is to assure that 'where id was, there shall ego be'. Has not reason a similar function in the larger sphere of the organization of mankind?

[1] Freud explicitly assigns to the ego the function of unifying and organizing. In accordance with the libidinal theory, however, he thinks it owes this power to the desexualized energy in which it had its origin. cf. *Inhibitions, Symptoms and Anxiety*, p. 33.

III

I propose next to comment briefly on the psycho-analytic theory of morals. There is an initial difficulty in doing this which arises from the fact that it is not clear whether what is intended is to provide, so to say, a natural history of morals, that is, to show how moral sentiments grow up in the individual, without raising the problem of the logical validity of moral judgements, or whether it is thought that this problem, too, can be decided by the psychological analysis itself. Dr E. Fromm, in an interesting discussion,[1] appears to think that it is possible by psychological methods to distinguish between what he calls genuine and fictitious ideals. In Freud's writings there is an underlying assumption, I think, that a rational ethic is possible, but it is not clear whether this will emerge, so to say, of itself when the myths of the nursery have been dissipated, or whether independent philosophical investigation is necessary in order to establish it. Professor Flugel,[2] if I have understood him aright, does not think that ethics can be reduced to psychology, but claims that psycho-analysis can throw useful light on the origin and growth of moral sentiments, even if it has to leave problems of ultimate validity to the philosophers. Following this lead we may ask what psycho-analysis has to teach us about morals from a purely psychological and sociological point of view.

In the first place, the psycho-analysts lay great stress on the fact that morality comes to the individual largely from without. He acquires it by a process which they call introjection or the incorporation into his mind of the standards and precepts upheld by impressive people in his environment. This, of course, is not new. What is new is the vigour with which they insist on the importance of early infantile experiences in the formation of character and the mass of evidence which they have accumulated in support of this view. While there can be no doubt that in this they have made an important contribution to moral psychology, it may nevertheless be suggested that they have tended to treat

[1] *Escape from Freedom*, 1941.
[2] *Man, Morals and Society*, 1945.

the family too much in isolation from the wider group and to neglect the pervasive influence exerted by society on the norms prevailing in the family. In other words, the authority exercised by the father is itself socially conditioned and its elucidation must lead back to an inquiry into the origins of social norms, of which those regulating life within the family form only a part. From this point of view psycho-analysis needs to be supplemented by a comparative study of the structure of the family and of different types of authority. Studies of this kind are as yet in their initial stages (Cf. *Autorität und Familie*. Ed. Horkheimer).

In regard to the content of morality psycho-analysts have for readily intelligible reasons tended to concentrate on the repressive aspects, that is, on negative injunctions or prohibitions. They have not given so much attention to the positive elements, that is, to what constitutes the good or worth-while. What is said about ideals is brought within the framework of the theory of the libido. The love of ideals is, in fact, reduced to self-love or 'narcissistic libido'. A portion of the libido is directed towards our real selves, but some of it goes not to ourselves as we are but to ourselves as we would like to be, in other words, to our ego-ideal. The ego-ideal is built up by identification with the father and later with father substitutes. In the course of identification these are idealized, we ascribe to them qualities which would make them worthy of love. The reason for idealizing loved objects is traced by Freud to narcissistic libido. 'The object serves as a substitute for some unattained ego-ideal of our own. We love it on account of the perfection which we have striven to reach for our own ego, and which we should now like to procure in this roundabout way as a means of satisfying our narcissism' (Group Psychology, p. 74). This, of course, leaves the nature of the search for our own perfection unexplained. But I find it hard to believe that the love of ideals is a form of self-love. Why should there not be other things or qualities which can be loved directly and for their own sake and not as parts of the self? The question should clearly not be prejudged in the interests of the libido theory.

The psycho-analytic theory is more novel and also more impressive in what it has to say on the negative aspects of the moral life. In the course of therapeutic treatment analysts were early struck with the great severity of the conscience, resulting in cruel self-humiliation and self-torture. To account for this, stress is laid on the part played by aggression in the formation of the super-ego. There is said to occur a recoil against the self of the aggression originally aroused by frustration and interference. In incorporating the authority of the parents into his own self the child also incorporates the aggression naturally attributed to the parent as a source of frustration, and at the same time the child directs his own aggression which he feels towards the parents in so far as they interfere with him, but which he has to repress, against himself. To this redoubled aggression is attributed the severity of the conscience and the fact that it often goes far beyond the severity of the parents.

In laying stress on the part played by unconscious factors in the growth of the conscience psycho-analysis has brought to light a mass of facts hitherto neglected by moral psychologists. It has shown in great detail how in the censure we direct against others as well as against ourselves our repressed impulses find an outlet. Self-deception or self-sophistication is a theme which great novelists have handled in their own way, before the days of psycho-analysis, and here and there moral psychologists have given the matter some attention. But no one has shown so clearly as the analysts how infinitely varied are the distortions to which the conscience is subject, in what subtle ways it can be affected by unconscious factors, and no one else has given such a detailed account of the mental processes involved. Perhaps in their eagerness to bring out the effects of unconscious aggression they have not given due weight to the repression of other impulses in the development of the conscience. A great many of the phenomena connected with self-censure may well be due to fear of one's own weakness and lack of self-mastery, and this, at least as much as displaced aggression, may account for the severity of the conscience.

The psycho-analysts lay great stress on the process through

which the individual moves from a stage in which authority is external to that in which it becomes an inward monitor. The transition is effected through what they call identification with the father. It seems to me that they exaggerate the extent to which the transformation from a morality of external sanction to one of inner acceptance is achieved by most individuals. No doubt in the course of social development moral teachers arise who preach that moral rules ought to be self-imposed and that what matters is not only the deed but the intention. But for many individuals even in advanced societies a great deal of morality remains prudential and conventional. People no doubt like to *believe* that their conscience is their own, but in this they are easily deceived. Where the transformation does occur it may be doubted whether it is due to the incorporation of the authority of the father into the self. An individualized and internal morality is much more likely to be built up in the course of our experience with equals with whom we have to establish a *modus vivendi*. It is in such experience that we come to recognize the objective necessity of rules and to accept them as such. Another important factor is the criticism of moral standards prevalent in his group which the individual may be led to make in the light of experience derived from contact with other standards and the clash of ideals which thus results. In this context, the psycho-analysts have tended to treat the family too much in isolation from the larger group and this has led them to underestimate the part played by social factors in the development of moral sentiments.

IV

It does not come within the province of this discussion to examine the validity of psycho-analytic theories within their own domain, nor am I competent to undertake this. I hope, however, that it has become clear from the outline given above that if psycho-analysis is to make the contribution to sociology which its great achievements have led us to expect its hypotheses need to be checked by direct study of social facts. The difficulty is, of course, that social phenomena are often the result of vast inter-actions which are not accessible to direct examination by psycho-analytic methods. Hence psycho-analytic explanations of these phenomena give the impression of being, so to say, imposed ready-made upon the facts, rather than elicited from them. A good example of this may be given from the way in which psycho-analysts have dealt with the problem of the causes of war. The theory of repression stood ready to hand. It was therefore plausible to formulate the hypothesis that unconscious tensions due to a faulty balancing of the repressive and repressed elements in the mind are among the deeper causes in predisposing states for war and in shaping its behaviour once it breaks out. The hypothesis is clearly legitimate and important. The difficulty is to find methods for testing its validity. No one has ever tried, so far as I know, to ascertain whether there is any relation between the amount and kind of repression of fundamental drives prevalent in a society and its readiness for war, nor to explain what happens to the unexploded aggression in societies that remain at peace, or who pass from a phase of militarism to one of peace. It would be interesting to know what is the psycho-analytic explanation of the fact that the Balkan peoples have been repeatedly involved in war, while the Scandinavian peoples have for a long period avoided it. Is there any difference in the amount of unconscious tension in the individuals composing these nations or in the statesmen that lead them? Is there any evidence to show that the infantile phases of mental development follow a course sufficiently different among these peoples to account for the difference in their behaviour? Until comparative studies of this kind become possible, I do not see that there can be any real evidence for the view that the most important causes of war are to be traced back to tensions in the individual mind of the kind that the psycho-analysts have disclosed.

Similar remarks apply, I think, to the attempts that have been made to explain movements like Nazism and Fascism in terms of psychopathology. Of course, the fact that the leaders of these movements were paranoiacs and sadists is of the greatest importance, since the concentration of power in their hands had the most terrible consequences. No doubt again the psychological analysis of the mental condition of those sections of the community which yielded most readily to their blandishments is highly relevant, since it is they who provided their leaders with the conditions which enabled them to satisfy their lust for power. Yet a movement like Nazism cannot be understood merely by penetrating into the minds of Nazi leaders and their followers, even if this could be done on a sufficiently large scale and by sufficiently reliable methods. From what I can gather from the evidence of psychopathologists whom I have consulted, the mental characteristics of the Nazi leaders whose records have been analysed could easily be matched from other countries where Fascism nevertheless obtained no hold. The differentiating factors are in all probability partly psychological, since countries differ in the extent to which the masses of the people are overcome by a feeling of powerlessness and anxiety and consequently become the ready tools of those who offer the means of escape. Nevertheless, the very same psychological factors may well find different expression under different economic and political conditions and, unless these are carefully studied and related to the psychological conditions, there is very little hope of providing an adequate explanation of large-scale social movements. The relations between psychology, including psychopathology, on the one hand and sociology on the other are thus extremely complex. The function of social psychology is, it seems to me, to show how the social structure and the changes in this structure affect the mentality of the individuals and groups composing the society and conversely how the mental condition of the members affects the social structure. The present condition of social psychology suggests that the most promising field of inquiry is the study of small groups. The strength of psycho analysis was in part due to its concentration on the interpersonal relations within the family. The study of crime also suggests that, where it is possible to make detailed case histories of individuals in their social setting, the psychological approach is enormously helpful. Yet concentration on small groups has its dangers. There is a tendency to forget that the tensions within these groups may well reflect the strains and stresses of the larger social structure of which they are a part, and that the character of the group is determined not merely by the interplay of the personal qualities of its members, but also by the traditions of the larger society. The latter, however, is not open to direct inspection by psychological methods. Herein lies the difficulty of social psychology. Its future development depends in the first place on improvements in the methods for observing group behaviour. But it also depends upon whether better ways can be found for linking its work with history and sociology than have so far been available.

On Prejudice[1]

THE WORD PREJUDICE is derived from the Latin *Prae-judicium* signifying a legal decision based on previous judgements or precedents. The etymology, however, is not very helpful in defining the present meaning. The term now has a derogatory implication, which obviously the legal term did not have, suggesting that there is something wrong or false about the judgement, and in any case, prejudgement is not sufficient to define prejudice. Many prejudices are not based on previous judgements and not all judgements so based are prejudices.

An examination of the ways in which the term prejudice is now commonly employed suggests that it may be provisionally defined to include (*a*) prejudgements (*Vorurteile*) or opinions and beliefs formed without examination or consideration and accepted uncritically when doubt or criticism might reasonably be expected; (*b*) beliefs or opinions influenced by logically irrelevant impulses, feelings, emotions, sentiments or complexes; (*c*) attitudes favourable or unfavourable towards persons or things formed prior to or not based on experience or knowledge of their qualities. Generally prejudice has a negative implication, being employed more frequently to describe unfavourable than favourable attitudes. 'Prepossession', on the other hand, which has a somewhat similar meaning, is used more positively to describe a favourable impression. It remains to be added that prejudice covers not only beliefs and attitudes but also the behaviour influenced by beliefs and attitudes.

[1] The third Jacques Cohen Memorial Lecture, delivered under the auspices of the Central Jewish Lecture Committee (Board of Deputies of British Jews) on 12 June 1958, at Friends' House, London. The lecture was also published in *The Jewish Journal of Sociology*, April 1959.

In order to understand the nature of prejudice it is helpful to consider first the psychology of 'certitude', that is, the state of feeling certain. This is a psychological term indicating a state of mind and is to be distinguished from 'certainty' which is best used as a logical term indicating that the grounds for a belief or judgement are logically adequate. We may feel certain of something which logically is false or at any rate without sufficient grounds. In current language we use several words to indicate degrees of certitude. We distinguish, for example, between knowledge, belief and opinion. I should not say that I believe, but that I know that I had porridge this morning or that two and two make four. 'Opinion', again, is used in reference to assertions which fall short of the assurance we have in knowledge or belief. 'It is my opinion that so and so is the case' means that I have some but not very full grounds for thinking that so and so is the case. The assent we give to opinions is milder, more open to doubt than that which we give to our beliefs. Opinion thus seems to be intermediate between knowing and doubting.

What then is this state of feeling certain and what are its conditions? The older psychologists, dominated by associationist theories, tended to explain certitude as the result of indissoluble associations. We believe two ideas to be necessarily linked if in the past they have occurred in contiguity or in immediate succession. Modern psychologists, though agreeing that invariable association is one ground of certitude, argue that it will account neither for the certitude of simple perceptions nor for the confidence we feel about axioms.

If dazzled by the sun I say 'It is light' the psychological necessity accompanying this assertion, though it is confined to a single instance is more absolute and immediate than that which is present when I say 'Unsupported bodies fall', a proposition which I and my ancestors before me have verified innumerable times and never known to fail.[1]

Similarly the degree of conviction with which I believe that

1 James Ward, *Psychological Principles*, p. 349.

things which are equal to the same thing are equal to each other is far greater than that which accompanies my belief that unsupported bodies will fall, despite the fact that the number of times in which I have actually experienced the connexion is far greater in the latter than in the former case. In both simple perception and the apprehension of objects or relations of a higher order, the conviction of certainty is immediate or intuitive, and, as it would seem, psychologically irreducible.

Perhaps the most general thing we can say about the state of certitude is that in some sense our mental processes are constrained or restricted. When we are convinced we are, so to say, overcome, compelled. I am convinced means I am forced to assent. This is most obvious in direct perception. If in broad daylight I open my eyes it is not in my power to decide whether I shall see or not. I am bound to see. Similarly we have only limited command over our organic sensations. I cannot get rid of a toothache by not attending to it. The certitude thus arising is of a primitive kind. We hardly ever think of questioning it.

Apart from direct perception, I may be equally certain about recent memory. I have no doubt at all about what I had for breakfast this morning; though if asked to give proof of the accuracy of my recollection I might be involved in difficulties because memory is notoriously fallible. Nevertheless, psychologically, immediate or recent memory has the directness of perception. In both cases the flow of my activity is restricted, my mental processes are determined for me. Wherever there is a similar restriction there is belief. In imaginative work, in writing a novel for example, you might think that you can shape what happens as you choose. But in so far as you do this you have no belief in the reality of the characters. If you believe in their reality you cannot make them do things which are not in keeping with their nature.

Following this line of thought, we may draw up a scale beginning with free fantasy such as you have in day dreaming, when the flow of your ideas is unrestricted and anything may come into your head, to imaginative construction where you have a good deal of freedom, but are still limited by the nature of your characters as you have conceived them, to the definite constraint which you experience in direct perception, in recent memory, in logical thought or in practical activity when the means chosen must be such as are in fact likely to achieve the ends desired. We can in this way classify mental processes according to the degree or kind of restrictions imposed on the mind. It will be noticed that dreaming differs from free fantasy in this respect. In the latter, objects can be moulded by your desires. In dreaming, on the other hand, the objects will resist your efforts and you may even struggle against them. This is why you believe in the reality of the objects while you are dreaming.

We must distinguish between implicit and explicit certitude. Normally when we take the trouble to say 'we are certain' we refer to statements which we might have doubted or which we had previously to ascertain or verify. In such cases the certainty is explicit. A great many of our beliefs are implicitly certain. We had no reason for doubting them. In fact what we call common sense or common knowledge consists of such implicit beliefs and they mostly remain unchallenged. Doubt arises when the conditions leave us freedom of choice, and we make some effort to find something which will help us to decide in favour of one of the alternatives. There is no virtue in doubting for doubting's sake. 'The ignorant man', Renouvier tells us, 'doubts little and the fool does not doubt at all.'[1]

The opposite to the tendency to doubt is credulity, that is readiness to believe without sufficient reasons. Of this, as we all know, there is any amount. For suspension of judgement a good deal of self-control is needed and active doubt requires sustained effort. It is easier to escape from the discomfort of uncertainty by stifling doubt and turning attention away from anything that might encourage it. Credulity is obviously an important factor in prejudice, as it is also of superstition. Superstition is a word difficult to define. In common use it means false beliefs concerning supernatural powers. There is often an implication that these beliefs are not only false but socially injurious, en-

[1] James Ward, *Psychological Principles*, p. 357.

couraging obscurantism and leading to cruelty. But this is disputed and what is injurious in certain circumstances may not be so in others.[1]

Another concept which has here to be considered is faith.[2] This is also difficult to define. It is commonly distinguished alike from knowledge and belief. In knowledge and belief we are constrained in varying degree by what is directly before us in perception or memory or the force of logical proof. In faith we venture beyond what is thus known to what is ideally possible. The stimulus to faith is often dissatisfaction with the world as we know it. But it is not mere dissatisfaction. At its best it is an adventure into the unknown and, though not knowledge, it is often a forerunner of knowledge and sometimes of knowledge otherwise unattainable. The relation between reasoned knowledge and faith is a well-worn theme and this is not the place for a detailed discussion. The rationalist will not close his mind to the suggestions of faith. He will realize that in the sense of anticipation of, and experimentation with, what is ideally possible, faith is an element not only in religion and morality, but also in theoretical and practical knowledge. But he will be on his guard against giving assent to conclusions to which we are prompted by feeling or desire alone, and against the dogmatic spirit which, not satisfied with believing, cannot rest until others believe as well.

Closely linked with the dogmatic spirit is fanaticism. Considering the havoc worked by fanaticism it is odd that psychologists have paid so little attention to it. It has generally been treated in connexion with the psychology of religion but, of course, fanaticism is by no means confined to religion. From the point of view of our present discussion it may be defined as an intensified form of the feeling of certitude. We can, I think, distinguish various types of fanatics. There is first the assertive or aggressive type. He is the sort of person who, filled with the sense of his mission, broods ascetically over his ideas and so establishes habits which make it impossible for him to consider or tolerate any

[1] Carveth Read, *Origin of Superstition.*
[2] cf. F. R. Tennant, *The Nature of Belief.*

beliefs that would tend to shake them. Such a person is often paranoid and, feeling himself to be persecuted, persecutes others. He is the persecuted persecutor. Obsessed by his ideas normal standards of conduct fail, and in support of his intense convictions he can indulge in the most terrible cruelties.

There is a second type into which the first passes by gradations. This is the type of person who is at bottom weak and unstable and not at all really certain. He has doubts which he dare not face. He will not admit that he is doubtful and to see others doubting infuriates him. He thus hunts his own doubts in others. He cannot believe so long as others doubt. Fearful and over-anxious, he seeks reassurance in exaggerated self-assertion. His weakness issues in destructive and cruel acts as terrible as those of the first type.

There is a third type which originates in excessive loyalty. Fanatics of this sort are people in whom loyalty is carried to an extreme. They tend to glorify their hero and their cause and to idealize their own devotion. They show their sensitiveness by intense jealousy for the honour of the object of their devotion. They will go to any length to avenge any doubt, slight or affront to their god, hero or cause. 'Crusades have been preached and massacres instigated for no other reason than a fancied slight upon the God.'[1]

The fanatic generally is jealous of his own importance, the dupe of his excited vanity, though often the intensity of his certitude is an exaggerated defence against his own doubt and anxiety. I have distinguished different types, but they have much in common and in their outward behaviour they may be very similar.

We must now try to define a little more precisely what is to be included under prejudice. In so far as the word relates to opinions and beliefs, it will be seen that not all wrong opinions and beliefs are prejudices. Errors arising through ignorance of relevant facts or through fallacious methods of reasoning are not necessarily due to prejudice. In so far as the term is applied to

[1] William James, *Varieties of Religious Experience*, p. 342.

attitudes again, it is easily seen that liking or disliking by itself does not amount to prejudice. If I like sugar and you do not I should not think of describing the fact by saying that I have a prejudice for, and you a prejudice against, sugar.

It would seem that what distinguishes prejudice is either the influence on our thinking of preformed judgements and the readiness to apply them to new cases without examination, when such examination might reasonably be expected; or else the influence on our thinking of logically irrelevant impulses, sentiments and complexes. The two modes of influence are closely connected. For feelings or desires may lead us to accept preformed judgements which in a cool hour we might be ready to doubt or at any rate hesitate to act upon. On the other hand, preformed judgements may induce feelings in us which otherwise we should not have experienced, as for example when we are unfavourably disposed towards individuals in advance of any experience of them merely because we know they are Negroes, Jews, Turks.

In analysing the conditions of certitude, it will be recalled, I have adopted the view that certitude involves the restriction or control of our thinking by conditions which are, so to say, forced upon us. This is most easily seen in the case of direct perception or in logical thought when we are carried away by the force of the evidence. Control of this sort may be called objective. But there is also control or restriction by subjective factors, as when our thinking is affected by our desires, passions or complexes. In the theoretical analysis of prejudice, we are concerned mainly with the way in which these subjective factors operate in generating prejudices and in making them readily acceptable once formed.

We may consider first the influence of preformed judgements. It is clear that prejudgement is normal and inevitable. We cannot be expected to start *de novo* every time we form a judgement. Indeed we could not do so, for we cannot proceed at all without the stock of ideas, categories, classifications, which we inherit in the very language we use. In what way then do preformed judgements encourage prejudice? I think the answer is to be found in two directions. In the first place, accepted beliefs and attitudes harden into habits and ingrained predilections and offer strong and often bitter resistance to change or the challenge of new experiences. This resistance is due partly to sheer inertia, partly to fear of the new, partly to vested interests and partly to group loyalty. It is only too easy to give examples. Some of the greatest discoveries, of the utmost importance to mankind, were denounced and opposed by contemporary authorities. Examples from the history of biology and medicine are Harvey's discovery of the circulation of the blood, the germ theory of disease, and more recently the teaching of psycho-analysis. Theological predilections have often hindered men otherwise open-minded and impartial from appreciating new advances in science. Legal reforms have rarely been initiated by lawyers and generally have had to overcome their apathy or active opposition.

In the second place, accepted beliefs contain not only the truths of experience systematized in common sense and science, but also the errors of misinterpreted experience, untested generalizations, and corrupted testimony and traditions. In so far as these erroneous beliefs were originally due to prejudgements and the influence of emotions they may be considered as causes of present prejudices. A great many prejudices are rooted in past prejudices. This is especially marked in the case of race prejudice, in which traditionally transmitted antipathies often provide the central core round which there gather other supporting antipathies constituting together an emotional system difficult to eradicate.

I come next to the influence of desires, feelings, and the systems formed of them. It is often said that we believe what we want to believe. This is true only in a certain sense. We cannot believe anything just by willing it. What happens is that when we want anything with a certain intensity our attention tends to be concentrated on those things which fit in with our desires and away from anything that does not. In this way every desire gathers around it beliefs favourable to it and diverts attention from conflicting beliefs. The strength of desires may easily blind us to the fact that they cannot all be realized, or that they are incompatible with each other. The range of knowledge at our command is here of great importance. A wide knowledge of the possibilities that are open and of the probable consequences of action may awaken conflicting desires and so make for hesitation or deliberation. In estimating consequences the strength of our regard for others may play a part. The weaker our interest in them the less is desire likely to be inhibited by its consequences to them and the less check on our beliefs tending to strengthen our desire.

Perhaps a more important factor in the formation of prejudices than specific desires are the more general dispositions described as 'interests'. Desires change with changes in the situation, but behind them are larger and more enduring needs seeking satisfaction in comprehensive ends such as health, home, family life, profession, etc., and forming the basis of the temporary purposes in the pursuit of which we are engaged from day to day. These 'interests' gather around them systems of beliefs congruent with them and repel beliefs not favouring them. As a source of prejudice group interests are specially important. For groups have common interests which may be opposed, or appear to be opposed, to the interests of other groups. These interests affect the beliefs and opinions of the group and colour their general outlook. Irrational factors here come into play. When group interests clash there is a strong tendency for beliefs to arise in each group attributing qualities to the other justifying the conflict. This is most obvious in war, but is easily discerned everywhere when groups of any size come into contact. Prejudices thus arising may be slight, fluid and transferable. But if they are sanctioned by social usages they may strike deep roots and issue in discriminatory treatment or even segregation, which then in turn strengthen the prejudices. Racial and ethnic prejudices afford numerous examples.

Passing now from the emotional background of prejudice to the cognitive structure of prejudiced beliefs, we may without any pretence to completeness enumerate the following features. These can be seen most easily perhaps in the case of racial or ethnic prejudice. Firstly, there is uncritical *generalization*. This

H

results in the attribution to all members of a group qualities in fact only observed in a few. Secondly, there is *specification*, or selective emphasis, that is the tendency to consider certain qualities as specially characteristic of a group which are in fact to be found equally commonly in other groups, e.g. when Jews are said to be ostentatious or pushful. Thirdly, there is *omission*, that is the tendency to overlook desirable qualities in the group which is disliked, or when they are too obvious to be denied to dismiss them as 'untypical'. Fourthly, there is *discrimination*, that is the tendency to condemn acts of one group which would be condoned or not noticed or even praised when committed by others, for example, when similar acts are considered as sharp practice in one case but regarded as showing business acumen in the other; or when Jews are condemned as 'money-minded' in a country where competition and the striving for money are considered proper and normal for everybody.

Other factors of importance are reliance on hearsay, suggestibility, self-deception, conscious and unconscious, sophistication and rationalization. Once the prejudiced beliefs are built up they tend to arouse emotions or passions similar to those which originally gave rise to them and thus to sustain or intensify them. They then impose themselves on the individual and become coercive and intolerant. The mass of beliefs thus engendered tends to be supported by other beliefs; for people like to think they have reasons for what they believe. In this way systems of belief are built up which are highly resistant and blind to doubt or criticism. The strength of prejudices like that of dogmas lies not in the reasoning on which they are based but in the mass of feelings behind them. Hence they do not yield easily to reasoning or even to persuasion.

To test this general analysis I propose to consider the case of racial or ethnic prejudice. This has been extensively studied by sociologists and psychologists and some general conclusions are beginning to emerge.

Prejudice, as we have seen, is ultimately to be traced to the influence on our beliefs of impulses or feelings. In the case of inter-group prejudices the central element seems to be the very deeply rooted and probably very ancient fear or dislike of the stranger. This fear normally leads to avoidance tempered by curiosity, but when groups of any size are thrown together the dislike does not disappear but tends to generate beliefs in justification and to be embodied in customs or modes of behaviour keeping the groups at a distance. Comparative study shows that the intensity of intergroup prejudice varies with the strength and persistence of this feeling of strangeness. Hence the importance of 'visible' criteria demarcating the groups and making them readily identifiable. The distinguishing marks may be physical, as in the case of the Negro in American society, or mainly cultural, for example, persistent patterns of behaviour or outward appearance, as in the case of the Jews in eastern Europe. The fundamental problem is to find out under what conditions the feeling of 'strangeness' or 'alienage' persists and under what conditions it yields to the forces making for social assimilation.

Given the element of alienage other sources of rivalry or conflict tend to take a group alignment. Thus, for example, economic rivalry between Jews and non-Jews would cause no more bitterness than normal business competition between individuals, if the Jew were not regarded as a stranger. The study of anti-semitism thus centres largely round the problem why the Jew has in the eyes of many remained a stranger even in countries where he has been settled for a thousand years. In the case of the American Negro the question is why it is that despite the adoption of typically American behaviour patterns and the fact that they have been longer resident in America than most white groups the barriers that perpetuate the minority status of Negroes persist. It would seem that the answer to such questions has to be sought in the history of the relations between the groups involved.

Closely associated with economic interests is the sense of social status and prestige. In many cases it becomes difficult to distinguish between race prejudice and class prejudice. The distinction between class and caste is of great importance in this connexion. Where caste-like distinctions prevail improvement in social standing or differentiation based on skill or training does not take an individual out of his group. On the other hand, in class societies vertical mobility is possible and individuals can rise in the social scale. This distinction has important consequences. In 'caste' societies group consciousness may be normally passive or quiescent, but in certain circumstances it may be intensified as, for example, when improvement in general standing can only be achieved through raising the status of the group as a whole. In class societies, on the other hand, there may be no need for united group action and consequently no intense group consciousness. This may account to some extent for the difference in the intensity of race consciousness as such in the United States of America, where caste distinctions survive, and, for example, Brazil, which has a class society. In Brazil class distinctions are closely associated with colour, but do not completely determine them. Wealth and education count. There is a Brazilian proverb, we are told, which says that a rich Negro is a white man and a poor white a Negro. No one would say this in the United States.[1] The influence of changing class relations on anti-semitism has not, as far as I know, been studied adequately. The rise of Jews in the social scale, especially when they move from country to country, tends to disturb class alignments. Hence the frequent charges of vulgarity, social climbing and the like, and the tendency in some countries to exclude Jews from the social amenities of the 'upper middle class', e.g. clubs or residential areas, and to set obstacles to the admission of Jews to occupations in which social status is a dominating factor. That there is a connexion between ethnic prejudice and class prejudice, is strongly suggested by various studies of anti-semitism in America and elsewhere.[2]

In an earlier discussion of anti-semitism[3] I suggested that it

[1] cf. 'Race Relations in Brazil', by Roger Bastide, *International Social Science Bulletin*, vol. ix, No. 4, 1957, p. 496.

[2] cf. R. M. MacIver, *The More Perfect Union*, p. 33.

[3] *Reason and Unreason in Society*, chap. x.

was necessary to distinguish different degrees of intensity in the feeling of antagonism or hostility and that the difference of degree may almost amount to a difference of kind. Studies of other ethnic antagonisms show, I think, that this distinction is of more general applicability. Group prejudices may be relatively mild, not founded in personal experience, but reflecting rather the attitude widely prevalent in a particular circle or group against other groups. The more intense kind of prejudice, on the other hand, depends more on the character structure of the individual. In this connexion psycho-analytic theories have made important contributions to the study of prejudice. They have shown that group prejudice may provide an outlet for inner tensions and anxieties and an object for displaced aggression, and they have accordingly given us various pictures of the types of person likely to be prejudiced. Theories of this sort may help to account for the peculiar intensity of prejudice in particular individuals, but are of lesser importance in dealing with group prejudice in general or with the various forms in which it occurs among different peoples or at different periods.[1]

There can be no doubt that ethnic prejudices differ greatly in kind and intensity. The relations between White, Negro and Asian in the United States differ from those prevailing in Inside the United States students of race relations distinguish various lines of demarcation. There is, first, the caste barrier which relegates all 'coloured' peoples including Chinese, Hindus, Japanese, Koreans, Filipinos, American Indians, Mexicans and some other Latin Americans to a lower caste. There is, next, what is described as a deep fissure line separating the Jews from the rest of the people. There are, thirdly, minor fissure lines detaching various other foreign-born, e.g. Poles, Czechs, Greeks, various Slavs, Italians and some others. In respect of all these there are variations in the intensity of discrimination and presumably in the underlying attitudes in different parts of the country and no doubt

[1] For a balanced account see Gordon W. Allport, *The Nature of Prejudice*, chap. 31.

in different periods of time. From the sociological point of view the important problem is to disentangle the conditions with which these variations are associated. A number of factors suggest themselves as *prima facie* likely to play a part. There is, firstly, the size of the groups in contact. 'Lest they multiply' is the cry already raised against the Israelites in ancient Egypt.[1] Where the dominant group is in a minority, as are now the Whites in South Africa, they are likely to fear submergence. Next, the sex ratio, especially in the early stages of settlement, may seriously affect subsequent attitudes. For example, in Brazil the Portuguese colonists did not at first bring their women with them (unlike the Anglo-Saxon migrants who emigrated with their families), and this favoured miscegenation. Thirdly, differences of attitude are affected by the extent of local concentration. Where migrants are concentrated in particular areas they tend to maintain their traditional patterns of living and thus to keep alive the sense of their difference from others. Where migrants are widely dispersed they are likely to come to terms more easily with the native population. This may act in different ways. When they are a conquering or in other ways a dominant group conscious of their superiority dispersal will incline them to seek for a certain solidarity, even though it may be of the condescending or paternalistic type. On the other hand, if the incoming groups feel weak they will tend, if widely dispersed, to abandon the struggle to survive as a distinct entity and to succumb to the forces of assimilation. Fourthly, occupational differentiation and the skill shown by the incoming groups to adapt themselves to new economic conditions strongly affect the attitude of the population to the minorities in their midst. Group prejudice seems to vary directly with the extent of competition for economic advantage or advance in social status. The operation of all these and other factors depends largely on the initial difference in cultural level, patterns of living and other factors giving rise to a sense of difference or strangeness. Given this strangeness, the forces making for conflict come to be associated with groups as such and to generate

[1] *Exodus*, i, 10.

group prejudices, needed to rationalize discrimination and perhaps, on the other side, to provide energy in the fight against discrimination.

It remains to be added that the factors making for group prejudice often operate in a circular manner. Thus in the case of the Jews the inner tendency towards isolation encouraged a policy of discrimination and discrimination in turn made for further isolation. Similarly, as has been argued at length by Myrdal, in the U.S.A. White prejudice causes discrimination against Negroes and keeps down their standard of living, and the low standards in turn stimulate antipathy and further discrimination.[1] Professor MacIver has described in more detail how the conditions produced by discrimination tend to sustain it. The group with greater power deprives the other group of the opportunities to social and economic advance. The upper group is thus strengthened in the sense of its own superiority. This in turn is reinforced by the factual evidence of inferiority that accompanies the lack of opportunity and the habits of subservience resulting from a policy of discrimination. In this way self-perpetuating complexes of conditions making for prejudice are created and sustained.[2]

Comparative study strongly confirms the view indicated above that although inter-group prejudice is found in one form or another in all societies of any size it is highly changeable in intensity and direction. This has been brought out very clearly by the highly detailed and elaborate studies that American investigators have devoted to the problem of the status of the Negro in American society. The results are strongly confirmed by studies of race consciousness in areas where it is less intense and where the changes which it has undergone have followed a different course as, for example, in Brazil. Historians have traced in detail the social and economic conditions which shaped Negro-White relations in the South and in the North after the emancipation from slavery. Equally detailed studies have been made of the impact of the two world wars on the status of the

---

[1] G. Myrdal, *An American Dilemma*, ch. iii.
[2] cf. *The More Perfect Union*, ch. iv.

Negro. Urbanization and northward migration have produced profound changes in the occupational structure of the Negroes, have brought into being a differentiated Negro middle class and enormously strengthened the power of Negro organizations to exert legal and political pressure against continuing discrimination. The social and economic changes due to the Second World War and perhaps also, the increasing use made in communist propaganda of the theme of racial tensions, have deepened the awareness of Americans of what has been called the American dilemma—the conflict between the persistent attitude to Negroes and the professed democratic ideals of American society. A new climate of opinion is thus being generated, greatly helped by the scientific work of sociologists and psychologists, more favourable to changes in the status of minorities and to a lessening of the intensity of prejudice against them.

There are differences of opinion about the extent and the depth of the changes that are occurring. Writing in 1948 Professor MacIver thought it quite possible that discrimination might be decreasing in some directions and growing stronger in others. It is sad to relate that in his opinion what he calls the deep fissure line dividing Jews from others was at that time holding firm, the more so in view of the more encouraging evidence of better relations in others.[1] In all cases the problem is to account for the sense of difference, strangeness or distance which is felt in varying degrees towards minorities and which prevents them from participating fully and on equal terms in the life of the communities in which they live.

I have dwelt at some length on the problem of ethnic prejudices because of its great importance at the present time and because it throws some light on the relation between psychological and sociological modes of explanation. Whilst the analysis of its cognitive and emotional structure is essential to an understanding of prejudice, such analysis will not of itself account for the collective aspects of prejudiced behaviour or for the changes which it undergoes under different social and economic

[1] *The More Perfect Union*, p. 46.

conditions. The tendencies towards uncritical generalization and the emotional sources of irrationality are always with us. What has to be explained is the form which they take when embodied in particular beliefs and directed to certain objects and not others. We need to discover the conditions which make for the wide prevalence of certain beliefs and give them a coercive character and which, on the other hand, bring about a general change in the climate of opinion in which even long-established prejudices tend to wither away. Problems of this sort cannot be fruitfully explored without considering the demographic, economic and cultural conditions. It is thus clear that both the psychological and sociological modes of approach are legitimate and necessary. From the practical or tactical point of view, however, it may well be that the analysis of social conditions may have prior or stronger claims. It is easier to change conditions than to alter feelings and attitudes, especially if these have deep roots in the unconscious mind. This is not to minimize the importance of psychological inquiry or of education.

Obviously everything should be done that can be done to reveal the irrationality of prejudices and to dissipate the myths that justify them. But such efforts are more likely to succeed if accompanied by outward changes in the conditions conducive to prejudice. Thus, for example, in the case of group prejudice, it is better tactics to attack discrimination directly, e.g. by efforts to raise the standard of living and to remove inequalities, than to try to change the feelings or attitudes associated with discrimination. No doubt, however, different types of prejudice have to be attacked in different ways. Dr Edward Glover in a study of War, Sadism and Pacifism gave it as his view that the first effective step towards abolishing war must be a complete investigation of the nature of the sadistic impulses and of the defence mechanisms tending to keep us unaware of their strength. It seems that the researches required would have to be very prolonged and be planned on 100 to 1,000 years' basis. A psycho-analyst writing in 1100 or 1200 might have been equally pessimistic of the possibility of abolishing private wars and establishing a unified system of public justice in Britain. But arguments of priority in these matters are unreal. Social changes are, as we have seen, frequently circular in their operation. When the circles are vicious it is sensible to try to break them by a simultaneous and concerted attack at different points.

Index

Acquired qualities, 87
Anti-intellectualism, xxx, 29
Anti-semitism, 178
Apathy of masses, 127

Bagehot, xxx, 20 *et seq.*
Baldwin, xxx
Barker, E., 52, 78
Barth, 62, 65
Behaviourism, viii
Belief, 168
Bosanquet, Dr B., 60, 106
 on general will, 67 *et seq.*
 on public opinion, 127
Bryce, Lord, xix
Butler, Bishop, vii

Certitude, 168
 v. Certainty, 168
Climate and national characteristics, xxix
Cole, G. H. D., 104, 140
Collective presentations, 46 *et seq.*
Common good, 78
Comte, A., xviii, xxvi
Conway, Sir Martin, 111, 114, 135
Crowd
 definitions, 111 *et seq.*
 low intelligence, 114
 emotional excitability, 115
Credulity, 170
Custom, 92 *et seq.*
 and law, 97
 and morals, 97

Desire, 32

Dicey, A. V., 126
Duguit, 100
Durkheim, 46 *et seq.*

Elections, 141
Engels, F., xv
Espinas, 44 *et seq.*
Esprit de corps, 53
Ethologists, views on instinct, ix

Faith, 171
Fanaticism, 171
Fashion, 92
Fletcher, R., x
Flugel, J. C., 160
Folk Psychology, xxviii, 85
Freud, S.,
 and 'anti-rationalism', xii
 on morals, 160
 sociological theories, 151 *et seq.*
 social justice, 153
Fromm, E., x, 160

Glover, E., 183
Good of whole and of all, 40–41
Guild Socialists, 131

Habit in society, 134
Hart, Dr, 25
Hegel, xxvi, 126
Hicks, Prof. G. Dawes, 29, 49
Historical School of Jurisprudence, xxvi, 98–99
Hobbes, xxv
Hobhouse, Prof. L. T., xxxii, 11, 12, 56, 80, 94

Horney, Karen, x
Human nature, xvii–xviii
Hurwicz, E., 90

Imitation, 23 et seq.
Impulse and will, 31 et seq.
Individual and group, 39 et seq.
Instinct
    and reflex action, 1–2
    and intelligent action, 1–2
    and emotion, 7
    and tradition, ii
    McDougall's theory of, 4 et seq.
Institution
    definition, 105
    and the individual, 109
    and social purpose, 106
    and spiritual life, 107–8

James, William, 172

Kant, I., xi

Lazarus and Steinthal, xxvii
Leaders, 135
    physical changes in, 138
    types of, 135
Le Bon, G., 111, 116 et seq.
Lloyd Morgan, C., 1, 9
Lowell, 122

MacIver, R., 53, 104, 144, 181
McDougall, Prof. W., xxvii, xxx,
    4 et seq., 13 et seq., 124, 142
    et seq.
    on group mind, 51 et seq.
Maine, Sir H., xxv, 96
Marxism, xv
Mutations and revolution, 102
Myrdal, G., 181

Nationality, 83 et seq.
Niebuhr, Rheinhold, xvii

Obligation, 99
Oligarchy, 136 et seq.
Opinion
    changes in, 126
Organic theory, 102 et seq.

Pareto, W., xiii–xv
Prejudice, 167 et seq.
    emotional background, 174
    cognitive structure, 175
    race prejudice, factors in, 176
        et seq.
    variations in, 179
Press, the, 120
Process and content, 45, 73
Psycho-analysis
    and morals, 160
    and Nazism, 164
    and social psychology, xxxi
    and war, 164
Public and crowd, 119
Public opinion, 122 et seq.
    value, 129 et seq.
    and general will, 123

Rationality, tests of, xx
Read, Carveth, 171
Representation
    psychological difficulties of, 137
        et seq.
    functional, 140
Ribot, 29
Ross, A. E., xxx, 113, 127
Royce, xxx
Russell, B., 108–9

Schmoller, G., 80, 124
Shand, A., 7, 14
Self, role in volition, 34
Sense and Thought, 30 et seq.
Sentiments, 33 et seq.
Social Mind, elements of, 58
Spencer, H. 88
Steinmetz,
    on national characteristics, 86
Stout, G. F., 6, 33, 34
Suggestion, 25 et seq.
Suggestion-imitation theory, 19
    et seq.
Superstition, 170
Sympathy, 27 et seq.

Tarde, 19 et seq., 122
Tender emotion, 14
Tennant, F. R., 171

Theories, influence on practice, 36

Trotter, W., 13, 16 *et seq.*

Unity, degrees of, in social aggregates, 56

Utilitarianism, psychological assumptions, xxv

Vinogradoff, Prof. P., 97, 99

Wallas, Graham, xxx, xxxii, 63, 111, 136, 142

War mood, 10

Ward, James, 170

Woodworth, Prof., 9, 10

Wundt, W.,
on custom, 92
on general will, 65 *et seq.*

DATE DUE

OCT 10 '66			
NOV 2 '66			
NOV 16 '66			
MAY 8 '67	MAY 8 '67		
OCT 23 '68	OCT 29 '68		
MAY 13 '71	MAY 13 '71		
DEC 1 2 '72	DEC 6 '78		
	APR 19 '78		
MAY 4 '78			
AP 5 '83	APR 21 '83		
GAYLORD			PRINTED IN U.S.A.